Also by Elizabeth Lewis

*Nurse Staffing and Patient Classification: Strategies for Success.* Lewis, Elizabeth N., and Carini, Patricia V. Aspen Systems Corporation, Rockville, MD. 1984. *Manual of Patient Classification: Systems and Techniques for Practical Application.* Lewis, Elizabeth N. Aspen Publications, Rockville, MD. 1989. Supplement 1991.

# BETWEEN OUR
# WORLDS

*The True Story of a Poor Peruvian Girl's*
*Impossible Dream to Become a Doctor and*
*How Our Journey Changed My Life*

*Elizabeth Lewis*

## ELIZABETH N. LEWIS

ISBN: 978-1-4834-8284-2 (sc)
ISBN: 978-1-4834-8283-5 (e)

Library of Congress Control Number: 2018903300

Lulu Publishing Services rev. date: 05/16/2018

For people everywhere who hold to a dream. Hold that dream tight to your heart, work hard, and never stop believing in yourself. The *how* will find its way to you.

# CONTENTS

Acknowledgments................................................................ix

Part 1:  A Troubled Girl with an Impossible Dream
Chapter 1    Two Elizabeths................................................. 2
Chapter 2    The Secret ...................................................... 9
Chapter 3    The Fall ........................................................ 20
Chapter 4    Truth ............................................................ 23
Chapter 5    Young and Troubled...................................... 26
Chapter 6    Standing Up.................................................. 31

Part 2:  Finding New Support
Chapter 7    Living Privileged........................................... 38
Chapter 8    Saying Goodbye ............................................ 44
Chapter 9    Decisions ...................................................... 52
Chapter 10   Visitor Visa ................................................... 60
Chapter 11   Etelvina ........................................................ 66

Part 3:  Goals Conflict with Memories
Chapter 12   Mission 2: Return to Arequipa...................... 70
Chapter 13   A Mission Almost Aborted ............................ 74
Chapter 14   Libreria Diana ............................................... 76
Chapter 15   Universidad Católica de Santa María............. 79
Chapter 16   Juliaca .......................................................... 81
Chapter 17   Carlos............................................................ 85
Chapter 18   Carlos Quispe? Where Is Carlos Quispe? ...... 88
Chapter 19   Tres Hermosas Chicas ................................... 91
Chapter 20   Sofia.............................................................. 93

## Part 4:  Change of Plans and Disappointment

Chapter 21    A Room With No View ..................................................... 98
Chapter 22    Team Dinner .............................................................. 102
Chapter 23    Kidnapped ................................................................ 105
Chapter 24    Leaving Arequipa ........................................................ 107
Chapter 25    Change of Plans ......................................................... 109
Chapter 26    Holidays................................................................. 116
Chapter 27    Disappointment .......................................................... 131

## Part 5:  Her Latin Heart Begins to Sing like a Bird

Chapter 28    La Taqueria de Carlito .................................................. 146
Chapter 29    Awakening ............................................................... 155
Chapter 30    Intern.................................................................. 158
Chapter 31    Graduation .............................................................. 172
Chapter 32    Condors Flying Free..................................................... 182

Epilogue................................................................................ 187

# ACKNOWLEDGMENTS

My family and friends have known parts of this story since it began, when I met Liz in 2004. They have watched me grow, as well as struggle with how to tell this good and true story. I am grateful for their support.

Marisha Chamberlain, poet, playwright, librettist, and friend, was a great help with editing the early chapters of this book. Marisha helped me make the young Liz come alive to the reader.

My friend and colleague, novelist Bonnie Hearn Hill, helped me find my voice to tell this story. I would not have been able to execute this work without her tough advice and insight.

Thank you to medical mission professionals throughout the world who travel and serve tirelessly to give the gifts of health and love to the poor and those in need of wellness and hope, particularly the Flying Samaritans International, Operation Smile, and Children's Surgery International.

A special thank you to the physicians, nurses and volunteers of CSI who participated in the 2004 and 2005 missions to Arequipa, many who actively supported Liz when she came to the US in 2005.

To the memory of Everett Anderson, who believed in a young author long ago.

Above all, I thank my husband, Tom, a published historian and passionate critic. Tom listened, read, and always offered encouragement, along with questions, criticisms, and points to ponder. As authors typically experience frustration and writer's block, Tom pushed me to not just put thoughts on paper but dig deep in my heart and capture my true and uncensored feelings in order to tell this story. Although all content of this book is my responsibility alone, this work is infinitely better for Tom's thoughtful commentary.

True Things

"True Things" Brian Andreas, StoryPeople, 1994

# PART 1

# A Troubled Girl with an Impossible Dream

They came to sit and dangle their feet off the edge of the world and after a while they forgot everything but the good and true things they would do someday.
—"True Things," Brian Andreas, StoryPeople, 1994

# CHAPTER 1

# Two Elizabeths

On a day in June 2004, two women named Elizabeth began their morning at the same hour, in the same time zone, but in different hemispheres. Northern Liz finished packing for a long airplane flight. Southern Liz put on her best professional clothes—a pair of worn jeans, a cotton blouse, and an ancient sweater—and set out walking. Two worlds were about to cross, joined by the helping hand of medical mission work. The question was, then as now, Who was helping whom?

I am the northern Liz, a nurse and privileged American. I was setting out to help offer corrective surgery to needy and impoverished Peruvian children with split lips and cleft palates. It was not my first service mission. I knew the days would be grueling physically and challenging emotionally. I also knew I was exercising a privilege. It was only because I have so much—financial means, learning, travel experience—that I could help. What I had to give was simple, really. I was returning because of the profound satisfaction I felt when applying my skills to make a difference. A child with a malformed face would smile.

I knew from the first moment I met Liz Cardona that ours wouldn't be an ordinary connection. She stood before me, clean and neat, less than five feet tall, with shining black hair to her shoulders. She wore jeans, clean loafers, and a white lab coat over her cotton blouse—no jewelry. She sported her name tag proudly: "Elizabeth Cardona, Interpreter." I was struck by her beautiful smile and her straight white teeth. She reached her tiny light brown hands out to meet mine, her palms up as if offering a gift.

She looked at my name tag that also said "Elizabeth" and, in a Spanish syntax I have grown to love, offered friendship.

"I see we have the same first name," she said. "I think that is a very good sign for us working together—don't you think?"

"Yes, I think you are right," I said and smiled at her as I extended both my hands to hers. I held her hands in mine for a moment and said, "And we will greatly appreciate your help interpreting for us."

Because most people in Peru are poor, I assumed that she was too. Yet she stood tall and moved with self-assurance. I heard confidence in her voice and saw determination in her dark brown eyes that followed mine as we worked together for the remarkable next nine days that would bond us for life. In those eyes, I felt the strength of this small young woman and, as I would come to know, her huge will.

Our medical group was Children's Surgery International (CSI), made up of thirty-two doctors, nurses, and other health professionals, most of us from Minnesota. The first two days would consist of screening potential patients. For the next six, we would perform corrective surgical procedures.

We had taken an overnight Continental flight from Minneapolis to Houston and then gone on to Lima. Following immigration, we boarded an hour-long Lan Peru flight to Arequipa in southern Peru, about one hundred miles north of the Chilean border. Arequipa's altitude is 8,800 feet, and as I stepped down from the plane, I felt light-headed.

"You'll get used to it," Mary Alice, the mission coordinator, said as we walked to the baggage claim. And she was right—we did. It was early morning. We were shuttled to the Casa Andina, a contemporary three-story hotel that would be our comfortable home for the next eight days. We quickly settled into our rooms and then met in the lobby to go to the hospital. Although we all had gotten little sleep during our nearly ten hours of travel, we were excited to finally be in Arequipa and ready to begin. Work always started quickly on missions. We were there for a purpose. Catching up on rest was a low priority.

People of Arequipa and other nearby communities and parents of children with cleft lips and palates had read about our mission in the local papers and heard of us on the radio. As a result, over the next two days, our doctors, nurses, coordinators, and interpreters evaluated more than two hundred prospective patients. We were scheduled to perform surgeries for six full days, and we knew that in that time we could perform only about ninety procedures. More than a hundred patients would have to be turned away and told they could return next year for a chance to be selected.

As our interpreter, Liz asked the parents how they'd arrived at the hospital. Most came on a bus from in or near Arequipa. Others traveled via car or bus from farther away. Some walked. Many arrived with several relatives and always with their other children. This was important because the greater the hardship was for the parents to bring the child to the screening, the more likely it was they would be selected for surgery since it was unlikely they could make the trip again.

Two or three surgeons carefully evaluated each infant or child, one at a time, to determine the potential outcome of the surgery. If the surgeons felt the outcome of the surgery was potentially optimistic, barring complications, the patient was put higher up on the list. If the patient had a fever or the surgeons felt a positive outcome could not be achieved in one surgery, the patient was put toward the bottom of the list. The days were long and challenging, and every patient who showed up was screened.

Nonmedical personnel created medical records, and the nurses documented the patients' vital signs. As our interpreter, Liz asked parents to tell us about the health of their children. She helped us check vital signs and marked our findings on the medical record. Volunteers photographed the children and made sure that their medical records moved along to the doctors who evaluated the children.

I noticed from the start that Liz appeared comfortable in this setting. She translated accurately, was graceful, spoke softly, comforted crying and fussy children, and put her arm around parents as she reassured them. She quickly identified what information we needed from the parents and explained the process. Liz was immediately a big help to us. She moved with confidence yet always watched me and followed my lead. In the midst of the busy, crowded, noisy room, our eyes met often. We smiled at each other, and I told her that she was doing a good job. Toward the end of our first day, there was a lull. I used this as a chance to talk to her.

"Thank you, Liz, for helping us," I said. "How did you hear about our group coming to Arequipa?"

"Yes, Ms. Liz, I will tell you about it," she replied. "Some weeks ago I saw the announcement in the newspaper. I also heard it on the radio and on the television, about the medical group that was coming to Arequipa to provide surgeries at no cost to children with the *labio de hendidura*, the split lip. I was excited to think that perhaps I could have an opportunity to use my English to help."

"It is good to know that our mission was well advertised. Did you have to apply with the hospital to be allowed to participate?" I asked.

"Yes, I did. I went to the hospital administrator, Mrs. Esmeralda García, and told her I wanted to volunteer to be an interpreter. But Mrs. Esmeralda told me you already had enough interpreters.

"I didn't think I would get accepted," Liz continued, "but I decided to show up at the hospital today anyway. That is when I met your mission coordinator, Mrs. Mary Alice. She heard me talking in English to one of your group, and she came over and told me that they were in need of another translator to work with the nurses caring for patients before they go to surgery. She was very kind. Then she brought me to you."

"Well, we absolutely do need your help, and we're glad to have you work with us, Liz!" I said. "My conversational Spanish is okay, but in the hospital setting, I need an interpreter like you to explain procedures and give postoperative instructions."

We were smiling at each other. I saw a girl with sad eyes, but when she smiled, her eyes came alive.

"You seem to be pretty comfortable with what's going on," I added. "Are you a student nurse?"

"No," she said softly as she looked down and picked up a patient chart, clearly not wanting to meet my eyes. "I have spent some time in the hospital. It is talk for another time."

She looked away and called out the name of the next patient. I continued to watch her and was puzzled. *Who is this young woman, and why do I feel like I want to know her? Like I need to know about her? She is beautiful and so caring, but when she is not talking with the patients, she looks sad.*

As the end of the day neared—after seven in the evening—I told her again, as did other nurses and doctors, how much we appreciated her help.

"We'll see you tomorrow morning, right?" I asked her.

She looked away. "Yes, I will be here, but I am not sure what time. I will do my best."

"Well, that's fine, Liz," I rambled. "We appreciate any help you can give us. We don't have enough interpreters, and your English is very good."

We shook hands. "Thank you again for this opportunity," she said, and this time she smiled.

"Our team needs to leave the hospital together through the front entrance where the cabs will take us to our hotel," I said. "Do you want to get a cab at the front door with us?"

"No," she replied. "I need to make some phone calls. You go on ahead."

"Okay," I said. "Well, thanks so much again. We'll look forward to seeing you tomorrow."

Liz turned away and walked in the opposite direction toward the hospital's rear entrance.

I recall clearly this first meeting as if it were yesterday, not the twelve years ago that it has been—the first day, the day that brought the two Elizabeths together, and for both of us, a day that made all the difference.

That evening, the medical team met at the hotel with all the charts of patients seen that day. Hours were spent deliberating and discussing which patients had the potential for the best outcome and which patients had the greatest hardship in getting here. The nonmedical team members brought in pizzas, soft drinks, and water.

Some very young children presented with poor nutrition that could cause postoperative problems, yet there was a high potential for a good outcome. Some children presented who were older, even twelve or fourteen, with only a cleft lip repair. The corrective surgery they needed was one of the simple surgeries that could be performed in less than an hour. Should the younger, malnourished child be given the surgery, or should we focus our attention on the older child who would be an easy repair and whose outcome would certainly be good? Doctors argued their rationales for their choices. Each doctor on the mission was there because he or she wanted to help as many children or young adults as possible, yet we knew that not everyone screened could be selected. These discussions sometimes became heated and continued long into the night as the drama escalated. Eventually, the doctors agreed to a tentative schedule.

It was also agreed that in six days, with the team and equipment we had, we could perform eighty-four surgeries, an average of fourteen a day. The next day's screening would finalize the schedule.

At the end of this first day of evaluating and discussing each patient, it was time for a long-awaited night of sleep. We were assigned to share a room with another team member. I shared with Dottie, a pediatric nurse at Children's Hospital in St. Paul. Dottie and I were both exhausted from a long day of travel and screening, and we knew that the next day would hold more of the same. We said good night, and the lights went out.

I lay awake thinking about the young woman who shared my name, the young woman with the sad eyes who seemed to turn into someone else when she was talking to parents or fussing over the children. I thought of calling my husband, Tom, as he would want to hear about our first day. I wanted to tell him about the Peruvian translator, but it was too late for a phone call.

I wanted to know more about Liz from Arequipa. Maybe at a break— if we even took a break. *Maybe during a lunch break we could eat together and I can ask her about herself. If she is not a nurse, why is she so comfortable with what we are doing? Has she participated in missions before? Sure ... that must be it. Other medical missions come here. She must be used to doing this.* I fell asleep exhausted. The six o'clock alarm beeped way too soon.

Dottie and I rushed to shower and dress. By six thirty, our team met at the hotel's restaurant, where we enjoyed a buffet breakfast of scrambled eggs, bacon, sausage, alpaca meat, cereal, platters of fresh fruit, and wonderful Peruvian coffee. The mission coordinators provided bottles of water and encouraged us to take several to keep handy in our backpacks. While finishing breakfast, there was enough time to greet others on our team and inquire about how everyone had slept and who ate the alpaca. Not surprisingly, alpaca is plentiful in Peru. On our missions, some loved it. I wasn't one of them.

Finished with breakfast, we gathered at the front of the hotel on Jerusalem Street and hailed taxis. Taxicabs in Peru are really small, subcompact Korean Ticos, and the drivers, or *taxistas*, own their own cars. We always went to and from the hospital in groups, with one of us in the front with the driver and three of us in the back squeezed together with little legroom, holding our bags and backpacks in our laps. While in these close quarters for the twenty-minute ride, someone always joked about which one of the men was taking up the most legroom. This time, the ride was in daylight, and we looked out the windows to read the billboards and watch the people along the streets. I saw a billboard with a picture of Alan Garcia, who would run and win his second election as Peru's president in 2006. *He looks like a jovial fellow,* I thought. *I wonder what, if anything, he stands for.*

We arrived at the hospital entrance and walked through much of the first floor to the screening room at the east side. By then it was seven thirty, and parents and children were already lined up. It was more of the same as the day before, but we would get used to the long days and intense work. None of us ever really talked about being tired; it's a fact of medical service missions. Everyone just worked through it, stayed focused, and kept a good attitude.

I looked around the room for Liz Cardona but didn't see her. I went into the hallway and looked both ways. No Liz.

I turned to Dottie and asked, "Do you see Liz, the interpreter who helped us yesterday? She said she was coming but didn't know what time, so maybe she got a late start."

"I bet she'll be here," Dottie said. "I bet she was tired and decided to sleep in for a while!"

"I guess you're right," I said as I turned, still looking for Liz.

Liz didn't show. We shared an interpreter with the intake and medical records team, but it went slower than the day before. Another eighty patients were screened. By early afternoon, we were becoming exhausted. My exhaustion was compounded by my disappointment that the young woman with the sad eyes hadn't returned.

# CHAPTER 2

# The Secret

The first day of surgery came quickly. Dottie and I were up at five thirty and met the rest of the team in the hotel restaurant at six o'clock. We all greeted one another as we dropped our backpacks at a table and shuffled through the buffet. The fresh fruit and undercooked scrambled eggs were my favorites.

Mary Alice, the mission coordinator, passed around the surgical schedule for the day. Fourteen cases were scheduled for the three surgeons—five cleft palates and nine cleft lips. One surgeon would do the five palates that would take two hours each, plus thirty minutes between cases, giving him a twelve-hour day. The remaining nine cases were shared between the other two surgeons. We knew that, typically, some cases would take longer. Some children bleed more than usual, and closing the palate can be complicated. This was to be expected.

After breakfast, we grabbed water bottles and went to meet cabbies on Jerusalem Street. The drivers from the previous days all knew we were good for tips, so the same ones awaited us every day. A cab fare from the hotel to the hospital was no more than five Peruvian soles, or about US$1.60. Ronald, a driver who showed up regularly, greeted us with the biggest smile I had seen since we had been in Arequipa. We thanked him for being so prompt. He responded in broken English, "Si, senora. I be glad to bring you to the Honorario Delgado Hospital." The Peruvian cab drivers had their pictures and cab numbers on an official-looking document mounted on the dashboard, similar to what we find in the United States. Ronald was smiling big for the camera the day his picture was taken, and I wondered what his story was. Each morning when we met the cabs in front of the hotel, I looked for Ronald. He was cheerful and prompt, and his taxi was larger than the ubiquitous Ticos.

In Peru, there are state-run, military, and a few private hospitals, where the wealthiest citizens seek care. Ours, the Honorario Delgado, is state run and looks much like other hospitals I have seen in developing countries. The lighting was dim because some burned-out bulbs hadn't been replaced, and the walls and floors showed wear. Chipped paint was noticeable on walls, beds, and equipment. Elevators sometimes worked, sometimes didn't. But for the most part, Honorario Delgado was clean and orderly. Housekeeping women mopped floors and cleaned windows nearly all day. The equipment was worn. Sometimes we, the Americans, rolled our eyes at the IV poles, which were often wooden poles with a nail on the side for the IV bag. I don't recall seeing any with regulators to monitor flow rates. The staff was generally cheerful and friendly, and we exchanged "Buenas dias" each morning. We were the Americans, after all, and they knew we were there to help their people. We were guests in their country, and we were sensitive to the conditions we observed. Yet too, there were often teaching opportunities when we were asked by the Peruvian nurses to suggest how to do a particular procedure or manage a piece of equipment.

Our surgeons had brought their own instruments. Any equipment they needed that was too large to manage on the flight had been shipped ahead of our arrival. The physicians were a bit nervous about the safe and timely arrival of their equipment, and this was the first thing they checked at the hospital when they arrived on day one of each mission.

Patients scheduled for each day's procedures were admitted the previous evening. A parent had to accompany each child, and usually it was a mother, but occasionally both parents attended. Siblings always tagged along since few people in Peru can afford babysitters. Children go everywhere with their parents.

The preop/postop unit where Dottie and I worked for the next six days was bustling with children running in the hallways and mothers calling after them. The third nurse was our team leader, Norrie, a Minneapolis pediatric nurse who speaks fluent Spanish. Norrie, a committed and seasoned mission nurse, was not scheduled for screening the previous two days, so she had just arrived in Arequipa the previous evening. That morning, she came to the hospital an hour before us in order to read the medical records of the fourteen patients scheduled for that day's surgery. She also wanted to make sure that Dottie and I had a translator in case she needed to serve in that role as well.

The Peruvian nurses and student nurses who would be working with us and learning from us were chattering and greeted us with smiles as we arrived in a room set up as a nurse's station. None spoke English.

"We're glad to see you!" Dottie and I said to Norrie, both of us grateful for her years of mission experience and her fluent Spanish.

"I think an in-country interpreter will be here too, at least for part of the time," Norrie said.

"Yes," I said. "During one day of screening, we had an interpreter named Elizabeth."

I no sooner got the words out when Liz walked into the room. Norrie, Dottie, and I smiled at Liz, and we all reached out our hands to welcome her. Norrie and Liz exchanged greetings in Spanish, and then Norrie gave the plan for the day.

"Elizabeth Cardona, you can work with Liz and Dottie and translate for them. Liz and Dottie, you can get the patients ready according to the schedule Mary Alice gave us. Surgery will send a student volunteer to get the patient when surgery is ready for them. When the children return from surgery, whichever of us is free can take postop vital signs."

Teamwork and positive camaraderie are probably the most important qualities a person can have when serving on a mission. Clinical skills are important, of course, but every participant has to maintain a "let's work together" attitude—at least if they ever want to be invited to participate again.

Liz promptly instructed all of us to call her Liz, and I did the same. From then and for the rest of the mission, I was Liz L. and she was Liz C.

Again, Liz C. jumped right in to help us. Dottie and I started taking preop vitals on the children scheduled next to go to the surgery suites on the sixth floor. Liz C. talked with the parents as we documented vital signs.

"Liz," I said, "please tell Mrs. Huahuamello that her daughter Nelida will be in surgery and recovery for about an hour and a half. Then Nelida will be brought back to her room. Reassure her that everything will be fine."

"Yes, I will tell her," said Liz C. And she did. When she finished, the mother turned to me. With tears in her eyes, she smiled and in a very emotional voice said, "Muchas gracias, Doctor. Muchas gracias." Many of the patients were native Peruvians who had been bused to Arequipa from Juliaca, a town high in the Andes very near Lake Titicaca, or another rural city, Puno. Although their native language was likely Quechua, five hundred years after the Spanish conquest, everyone understood Spanish. Most had never been in a hospital. To them, our white lab coats meant we were all doctors. We seldom straightened out what our roles were. It didn't matter.

The morning sped by, and we stayed on schedule. The infants and young children came back from surgery, and most cried until their mothers held them. The infants could not nurse from their mothers just yet because of the oral surgery. The mothers fed them from bottles or syringes.

Liz C. was engaged with the children and the parents and helped the mothers feed their children. She looked to Dottie and me for instructions on what to do next. I was still curious about why she hadn't come to screening the previous day, but she didn't bring it up. I didn't either.

I don't have children. It was a conscious decision on my part. I had a fifteen-year span between marriages, and my career and graduate school were my priorities. I held senior management positions in hospitals and health care organizations. My life was rich and rewarding, and not for a minute did I ever wish for children in my life. Seeing the realities of overpopulation and poverty only confirmed that my decision was right for me.

However, seeing the look on a mother's face when she sees her child for the first time following the cleft lip repair is touching, as a parent or a health care professional. Liz C. and Dottie adored the children. They both held and rocked the infants after surgery or knelt down to the level of a two-year-old and spoke comfortingly, Liz in Spanish and Dottie in English. It didn't matter that the children couldn't understand Dottie's English. It was the same with the surgeons. Some spoke Spanish well and others not at all. But all the children and parents understood their caring.

I had learned to speak some Spanish during my missions to Baja, California, in earlier years, as well as in Colombia. I struggled but enjoyed speaking my best Spanish to the mothers about their families and where they lived, answering their questions and reassuring them. The mothers would almost cling to Norrie, Dottie, or me and sometimes followed us closely. With Liz translating, they told us they loved us, that we were angels, and that God would bless us. It was sweet.

At one point I thanked Liz for telling us all the thank-yous from the mothers, particularly from Mrs. Huahuamello, but that they did not need to keep telling us how wonderful we were. I added that this was why we were in Arequipa—to help people. Then Liz politely set me straight.

"Ms. Liz, some of these people are from high in the Andes near Juliaca. They are native people, and they are very poor. They are—how you say—they are in awe of you and your group. To them, your group has saved their children from a life of pain and sorrow by fixing the lip or the palate. They are expressing their love and gratitude. They have nothing else to give you but love."

I turned to Liz and saw tears in her eyes.

"Liz, I'm so sorry," I said, and I put my arm around her shoulder. "That was insensitive of me. I know you're right. Thank you."

I realized how American I had sounded. Peru is one of the poorest countries in Latin America. These children and their families were among the poorest of the poor with little access to health care—certainly not to the kind of surgeries we performed. We are bold and assertive because we have knowledge, experience and money—mostly money. I was humbled. I learned something about poverty that day.

By noon, Norrie, Dottie, and I agreed that we would each take a half hour separately for lunch and to get off our feet.

"Will you join me for lunch, Liz?" I asked. "I'm hungry. How about you?"

Liz diverted her eyes. "Yes, I will join you, Ms. Liz, but I am not too hungry. I will have something to drink, however."

"Good, then we'll have lunch." I was wondering if Liz's comment was because she had no money.

I got my backpack, and Liz and I started walking toward the hospital cafeteria. As I put my arm around her shoulder, I realized that she was even shorter than I am at five foot two. "Thanks again, Liz," I said, "for helping me understand about Nelida's mother, who was just grateful. I really appreciate it. This is my first time in Peru, so I'm learning."

"That is no problem," Liz said, putting her arm around my waist.

"The poverty in my country is a complicated thing. I will help you understand it, Ms. Liz."

"You don't have to call me Ms. Liz. Liz is good."

"Well, then we will be calling each other the same name, but at least *we* will know who we are talking to, isn't that right!" Liz said with a big smile.

"Yes, that is exactly right!" I said, and we both laughed.

For the first time, I saw Liz's beautiful smile, which lit up her dark eyes. In that moment I saw no sadness.

In the hospital cafeteria, employees in scrubs and white uniforms sat in groups of three and four, chatting and eating. There were plenty of available tables. The food choices were ham sandwiches, lettuce salads with tomatoes and cucumbers, and empañadas—a light pastry filled with cheese, beef, or potatoes that I learned to love.

I ordered cheese empañadas and bottled water. When Liz hesitated, my instinct said she might not have money.

Quickly, I said, "Select whatever you like, Liz. It's my treat."

"Thank you, Liz," she said softly as she also selected the cheese empañadas, along with an Inca Kola, a very sweet, brilliant yellow Peruvian bottled soda whose slogan is "El sabor del Peru," or "The taste of Peru." We found a table. It felt good to sit.

I had many questions, and it was hard to know where to start. I decided the poverty topic would be a good place since she had offered to tell me about it.

"Tell me more about poverty in your country," I began. "I've been on missions in other poor countries, like Mexico and Colombia, but never talked about it with the people in that country."

"I do know that there is poverty in the United States, but it is different here because it is the predominant way of life. Most people in Peru are poor and with no opportunity," Liz said. "Many people who live in poverty in my country are angry. They think that they are, as you say, the victims and that they are owed a living by our government. They are often very unhappy, and they misbehave. They will drink too much, and they are not always nice to their children or the men to their wives. If they lose their jobs, they become angrier. They have accepted this behavior through the generations. They know no other way."

"But Mrs. Huahuamello doesn't seem angry, and she seems to love her little girl," I replied.

"Yes, you are right. She is different. Mrs. Huahuamello is a native Peruvian, and she and her family live in the high country. They are poorer in the remote areas of Peru than in the cities, but they have a different attitude and different cultural rules and beliefs. In spite of being poor, they are very proud and do not want to accept the handouts. This is why Mrs. Huahuamello was so grateful. She is not angry in her poverty. She is grateful, and she has love in her heart. She wanted to give that love to you. You will see that there are very different ways that people in my country learn to live ... to cope with living in poverty."

"I think I understand," I said. But what I was thinking was that Liz did not sound like a young person, perhaps in her middle twenties, but rather like an older woman.

Before I thought about it sounding presumptive, a question just came out: "How do you feel about living in poverty, Liz?" *Oops. Did I shock her by being so blunt?* After all, she had never said *she* was poor.

"Well, I have known no other way of life," she said without a change in expression. "It is the usual condition in my country. The majority of people are poor. There are some differences in—how do you say—the amount, the levels of poverty. Is that the right way to say it?"

"Yes, that's right. There are differences in the extent of poverty between people or families. Is that what you mean?" I asked.

"Yes, that is it. Sometimes I have trouble to think of the exact word." Liz smiled. "So I am grateful for getting help to find the right word. Anyway, my family was poor and they have always been without many of the necessities, but you know, they get by. I get by with very little. I do not need fancy things; I am more interested in books and learning than clothes or things of expense. It is what you learn to cope with when you don't have nothing. I try to live the best I can and do the best I can do with what I have."

"I understand. There is poverty in the United States too. And I know both of these attitudes exist. It is helpful to hear you explain this so well," I said. Then I changed the subject.

"Where did you learn to speak English so well—at school, or did you take English in college?"

"I knew as a young girl that learning English would help me no matter what I did in my life, so I studied English whenever I could. I began to learn to read and speak English when I was five years old. I looked for books in English. I listened to the English channels on the radio and, when I was older, the television. Then later I took English classes. I have also studied at a university in Lima, so I am qualified to teach English as a second language to secondary school students. And I do that whenever I can."

"Well, you do a great job!" I said. "Do other members in your family speak English?"

"No, they do not," Liz said as she looked down at her empanadas.

We ate in silence for what felt to me like a long pause. Did my asking about her family trigger something that she did not want to discuss? I saw the sad look again in her dark eyes. I was going to change the subject again, but apparently Liz didn't want to.

"My family is a complicated thing, but I do fine on my own," she offered.

"That's good. Do you live here in Arequipa?" *What a stupid question,* I thought the moment it came out. *Of course she lives in Arequipa. She just told me she was poor. Do I think she commutes here from Lima?* She continued, and her conversation put me at ease quickly.

"Yes, I do. I live in an apartment that is owned by my uncle. Well, he is not really my uncle, but he is the person who has been the unconditional person in my life since I graduated from the secondary school. He is Carlos. I have always thought of him as my uncle."

"Are you in school now?" I asked.

"No," she said, looking sad again. "I have attended the medical school classes at the St. Mary Catholic University here in Arequipa. You see, since I was a young girl I have had a dream to become a doctor."

"Oh, that's wonderful! How far along are you in medical school?" I asked.

"I have completed two semesters, but I had to drop out."

"Was medical school difficult?"

Liz paused for a long time. "Well, yes, it was, but that was not the reason. I had to keep working to pay for school," she said.

"I know that medical school can be a long and expensive commitment in the United States. Is it like that in Peru also?" I asked.

"Yes. I was able to take out a loan to attend medical school, and my uncle helped me too, but there was more to it, and then he could not help me anymore. Now I am working as a tutor of biology and also as an English teacher so I can pay off the school loan and try to make enough money so I can receive my grades and register for another semester."

"I'd like to hear more about this, but let's get back to the patients now. Are you able to have dinner tonight? We both have to eat, so if you're available, I'd like you to join me," I said, hoping to put the worry about who will pay out of her mind.

"Yes, I would like to talk to you more. I can do that. At least tonight, I can."

At eight o'clock, we finished the surgeries for the day. Liz and I took a cab to Aryquepay, a restaurant just down the street from my hotel. Liz suggested the restaurant because she said the food was authentic Peruvian and it would be a good place to talk.

Once in the restaurant, I ordered a Pisco sour, a Peruvian favorite made with Pisco, a popular Peruvian grape liquor, mixed with lime juice, egg whites, and bitters. Liz ordered the same.

"So tell me more about you, Liz," I said, "your time in medical school, and about your family too if you want to."

Liz folded her hands on the table as we waited for our drinks and looked hard into my eyes. At first she was cautious and deliberate when she spoke. Over the coming days and evenings at dinner, I earned her trust. And I heard a story that would pierce my soul.

Liz Cardona was born in Arequipa. While Lima is the capital of Peru with more than 8 million people, Arequipa is the second-largest city with a population of 1.2 million. Arequipanians are a proud people who refer to Arequipa as the cultural capital of Peru. They boast of Arequipa being the White City, and it justly deserves its nickname. Much of the city center is built of sillar, a white volcanic stone. Three volcanoes tower over the city—Chachani, Misti, and Pichu Pichu. Periodically, there is volcanic activity.

At an altitude of 8,800 feet, Arequipa is nestled between the Pacific Ocean and the magnificent Andes. Its population includes a small mixture of white Spanish people, many native Indian Peruvians, and mostly Mestizo, a mix between the Spanish and Indian people. I learned that although Liz describes herself as Mestizo, she has many physical characteristics of native Indian Peruvians. The Spanish Peruvians as a rule are wealthier. The Mestizo and Indian Peruvians are poorer, and this is typical throughout Peru and much of Latin America. The climate in Arequipa is mild by Midwest US standards, and the sun shines most every day.

I learned that the sun did not shine nearly so brightly on the life of the young Liz. "It is complicated," she said.

When Liz was born, her mother, Sofia, was twenty years old and her father, Mateo, thirty-seven. They were divorcing when Sofia learned she was pregnant. Sofia was already burdened with a three-year-old daughter, Marianna, and the infant Elizabeth only complicated Sofia's life. To make her own life easier, when Liz was five months old, Sofia gave her to her parents, Liz's grandparents, Etelvina and Aurelio, who lived in Aplao, an outlying city of about thirty thousand people but within the district of Arequipa. Etelvina and Aurelio were in their midfifties. Etelvina was slight with small bones but was strong enough to work on the family farm. Aurelio was short with premature silver hair. Liz spent the first six years of her life in Aplao believing that her grandparents were her parents. They had two children of their own, boys who were eleven and fifteen years old when Sofia brought Liz to live with them. Liz remembers that they were not particularly close as a family, but she loved them very much. Their home in Aplao was humble and simple. Clay blocks formed the walls, the ceiling was thin layers of metal construction, and the floor was compact ground—a dirt floor. While most of the town had electricity, they had none. The water that Etelvina used for cooking came from the river. As many families in Aplao, they were farmers and raised sheep and crops, including potatoes, tomatoes, onions, oranges, and apples.

Liz lived her first six years with her grandparents, never knowing her real parents existed. At four, Liz had daily chores on the farm. Each morning, she would wake at six o'clock and spend the morning tending to the sheep and doing whatever Aurelio told her to do. Liz's great-grandmother, Jimena, Etelvina's mother, was often at Etelvina and Aurelio's home.

Liz said, "Jimena used to yell a lot at everyone, but I did not know why." Liz did not like Jimena and tried to find something to do when she was at their home. "My grandparents were in their ignorance. They repeated how their parents treated them. Like I told you earlier, there is a cycle of poverty in my country, and this is not unusual. Poor people are usually very sad and often angry and ignore or mistreat their children. This is just a part of our culture of poverty."

As Liz grew up, she came to believe that being disrespected or ignored by adults was an expected way of life. "My grandfather thought that he was a kind person. He had no idea how to behave otherwise. I was so young that I did not know any other way of life until I was much older. I thought that all children were just ignored and mistreated and this is just a part of everyday living."

The house in Aplao had a small balcony where young Liz would go every day to sit and look at the sunrise and farming landscape. At four, Liz fantasized about what her life would be like with people who showed her love and kindness.

Liz said that her best times when she lived with Etelvina and Aurelio were when she attended school. When her morning chores were done, Etelvina would take four-year-old Liz to the only school in the community. She sat in the back of the classes and began to learn to read, write, and do basic math. She formally started school when she was five, but most of the students were older. Formal education was unstructured. Parents often needed children to work on the farms, so children were put in schools when it worked best for the family and the farming responsibilities.

"When I was five years old I was a thoughtful and serious little girl. I think this was because I did not feel love in my life and I was alone most of the time. I learned some basic math and learned to read the newspapers because it made me feel good. I attended the school at the age of four and five just for fun, and it was free. In Aplao children attended school at different ages. The people were poor, and they did not have money or an economy to support education. The people were more interested in teaching their children to grow the land instead of going to school. I wanted to attend school very much. I think it was an escape from my sadness and my hope for being loved. I felt that my grandmother let me go to school so I would be out of her way."

# CHAPTER 3

# The Fall

On a bright, sunny morning when Liz was five years old, Sofia's older sister Nellie, her husband Victor, and their two boys drove from Arequipa to Aplao to visit Nellie's mother Etelvina. Nellie and Victor were Liz's aunt and uncle and their children Liz's cousins, although she did not know it at the time. Etelvina and Aurelio took the family to the small village of Pampa Chara near the Majes Valley, one of the deepest canyons on earth. The area offered a mild climate, spectacular scenery, and an enjoyable place for picnicking, playing, and exploring. The children played while the adults ate, relaxed, and talked.

The four boys, all older than Liz, did not want to play with her, so Liz wandered away alone. The terrain was rugged, but Liz wanted to explore. She came to a rocky cliff, and while it was fenced off, Liz was curious and walked to the edge. She remembers how beautiful it was.

"As I looked over the edge of the cliff, I thought, *How far down is it? If only I could fly like a large condor through this valley and fly away from the prison of sadness in my life.* There were many cactus plants below the cliff, and I started to play a game where I would throw a stone and try to hit a particular cactus. Two times, I hit one that I had pointed out in my mind. I was having fun when, the third time, I lost my footing, slipped, and fell through the fencing. I remember it felt like a very long way, and then I landed hard. I must have become unconscious. When I woke up I was in the middle of a sharp tree, and I could not move at all. I was frightened, alone, and helpless. I thought, *God, please help me. I am in your hands.* Then I heard someone yell, 'Mrs. Tobina's child has fallen through the fencing!' "

Nellie's husband Victor climbed down the rugged cliff side to the wounded and disoriented Liz. It felt to Liz that it took forever for Victor to reach her. He pulled her from the tree, carried her up the cliff side, and covered her with a blanket from his car. Liz was bleeding badly from multiple wounds. By then, the sunny skies had turned dark and it began raining. The group took Liz back to Etelvina's home. The injuries were serious. She had open wounds on her back, neck, and head and multiple bruises and cuts. Later, she learned she had injuries to her spine and torn muscles and tendons on her left leg. Although Aplao was a district of Arequipa, Etelvina and Aurelio's farm was remote. It was 1978, but little health care was available to the poor, so Etelvina and Aurelio cared for Liz.

Unable to walk, Liz was confined to bed. Blood oozed from her gashes for days. Liz recalled that she often cried from the pain.

Then, a hero came into Liz's life. Juan Medina was his name, as Liz recalled years later with her grandfather Aurelio's help. He was a local caregiver, perhaps a doctor. Liz remembered that he wore a white coat and carried a bag with medicines and supplies he used to clean her wounds. "I thought he was a doctor because in my young eyes he looked like a doctor. I was young, but I remember Juan Medina like it was yesterday. Years later, my grandfather told me that Juan had learned from people in Aplao that a young girl had fallen from a cliff and had severe injuries."

Juan cleaned and dressed the bedridden Liz's now-infected wounds. He injected antibiotics and painkillers. Thereafter, Juan Medina came daily to visit his young patient. As her wounds began to heal, he taught Liz how to clean and dress them. He worked with her daily to rehabilitate her weak muscles. Over a period of months, with Juan Medina's comfort and support, Liz learned to walk again.

Today, Liz still has large red scars on her left leg, reminders of the accident that Sunday afternoon in the Majes Valley. The scars also remind her, she says, of the lonely life she lived in Aplao. When Liz recalls that Juan Medina saved her from permanent and debilitating effects from the accident, she also remembers that her caregiver did something else. The kindness and compassion that Juan showed her stayed with her. When I saw Liz caring for the patients during our mission, I was struck by the gentle kindness that seemed to come so naturally to her. During our talk about the accident, Liz reminisced about the details of her recovery that were so very clear in her mind.

"Juan Medina saved my life. Everyone thought that I would not recover, that I would die because I was so tiny, thin, and fragile. Juan Medina gave me a will to live and also left in me a very strong memory. It is that memory that made me want to become a doctor. As I got older I thought how amazing it would be if I was able to do the same thing for someone else as he did for me. So you see, dear Liz, in some ways Juan Medina saved my life twice."

# CHAPTER 4

## Truth

Over the coming days and into the evenings when we finished caring for the children, and when Liz was able to stay, we would go to one of the restaurants on Jerusalem Street near the Casa Andina. We were comfortable together and were becoming friends. She asked me where I lived in the States, about my family and my work. I told her about Tom, my husband, and some of the things we liked to do. She asked if I had parents living, and when I said they had both died, she was interested in hearing about them and our relationships. She smiled when I talked about my loving parents. She asked me if I had siblings and was interested in hearing about my brother Mark, asking if we were close. I told her about my niece Jenny and her then two-year old boy Charlie. Liz delighted in hearing about the antics of a two-year old. She smiled and laughed, almost as if it were an escape from talking about her own story. I realized how sad her life was compared to my uncomplicated and privileged life.

"Your accident and your long recovery sound like a very painful and difficult time for you. What was your life like in Aplao when you finally recovered fully?" I asked.

"Yes, Liz, it was very difficult. It was nearly a year. I had hoped to be able to go back to school, but instead, my parents, Etelvina and Aurelio, received the news and I will tell you about it."

At the age of six, Liz looked forward to returning to the chores on the farm and to attending the nearby school. Part of her enthusiasm for school was to be away from her sad life with Etelvina and Aurelio, whom she believed were her parents. Since she had met Juan Medina, she had a new excitement. As an adult, Liz said she did not truly understand her love of school and learning when she was a young girl, but she knew school was going to be important to her.

Etelvina's mother, Josefa, lived in Aplao and visited Etelvina and Aurelio often. Liz recalls that when Josefa came to visit she would yell a lot. One day when she was visiting, Josefa revealed the secret.

"Etelvina and Aurelio are not your real parents!" Josefa said loudly. "Your real mother gave you away to your grandmother, Etelvina."

Etelvina and Aurelio interrupted. "No, no! Do not tell her that. We are your real parents, Liz. What Josefa says is not true"

But Josefa insisted. Liz told me, "It was hard for me to believe that Etelvina and Aurelio were not my parents. I was only six, and I could not understand why my real mother would give me away. I remember crying."

Liz learned that Sofia had recently told Etelvina that she wanted Liz to come back to Arequipa to live with her, her new husband Jesus, and their two daughters—Lydia, age three, and Joane, age one, who were Liz's half-sisters. Josefa and Etelvina argued, and Josefa said the secret had to be revealed because of Sofia's demand to have Liz returned.

Within days, Etelvina took Liz to Arequipa to meet Sofia and her second husband. There, Liz met her older sister Marianna and her half-sisters for the first time.

"You can imagine how confused I was. I was only six years old, and hearing the truth about the secret that had been kept from me was a heartbreak."

When she first met Sofia, Liz refused to speak to her or Jesus. Etelvina tried to explain to Liz that Sofia was her real mother and to give her a chance.

Sofia intended that from this first meeting, Liz would stay with Sofia and Jesus in Arequipa. She tried to be kind to Liz, but six-year-old Liz was angry and confused. As Liz shared her story with me, tears welled up in her sad brown eyes and streamed down her cheeks.

"As a young child, I had such a lonely life. Then I learned that the people who raised me were not my parents and that my real parents gave me away. I could not understand it. I think that the reason I did not like Josefa was because she told me the truth about the secret. I used to dream about being with people who loved me. Then the day came that I met my mother. When I talk about it here with you, I feel a pain in my heart. I have not been back to Aplao since I was six years old, and I don't think I could go there again. Meeting my mother was the saddest day of my life."

# CHAPTER 5

# Young and Troubled

Each day when our work was completed, Liz and I continued our conversations at the restaurant on Jerusalem Street. One evening, Liz told me her story of growing up.

"When my grandmother Etelvina took me to Arequipa to meet and live with my mother, it was my first visit to the civilization, which is what we called the city. She prepared me, but I was angry, and even at my age I could not understand how my mother could have given me away." On this cold winter day in southern Peru, Sofia took six-year-old Liz from the only parents, the only home, she knew.

"At first, living with my mother and Jesus was a strange world to me. I did not like it at first, but I got used to it. What could I do? My mother and Jesus had a small house. It was nothing special. My older sister, Marianna, who was nine, and I shared a tiny bedroom. Lydia, my younger stepsister was three and Joane was only one, and they stayed in another room. Joane was still a baby, and Lydia had to help take care of her."

Liz went on to say, "Education in Peru is free and required for the primary and secondary levels. Primary level is attended by students who are the ages from six to twelve for six years. Secondary level is what you call in the United States the high school level and is taken for five years by students from twelve to seventeen years. My mother enrolled me right away in school.

"I was content because I could go to the school every day. But my mother ignored me mostly, so I wondered why she wanted me to live with her. It was still very confusing, and I thought my sadness and loneliness was just part of being a little girl. I grew closer to my sister Marianna and hoped that maybe when I was her age I would be happier.

"At the age of seven, my mother took me on the twelve-hour bus ride to Lima to meet my father for the first time. This visit felt like more of the same for me. I was still very confused.

"My father, Mateo, is a complicated person. He is seventeen years older than my mother and had a secret life before he knew her. He had been already married and had three children, but my mother did not know about this. My father was of native Peruvian decent with some of the same facial features as Marianna and me. My mother and father were on speaking terms when we made the visit, but not much more than that. They took me to the Estacion de Cieneguilla y su Mundo Magico, a national park in Lima. The visit lasted for the weekend and then my mother brought me back to Arequipa. The visit was okay, but I did not have any particular thoughts about my father one way or another.

"I continued in the primary school and I liked it—the classes and the learning. I grew to love my sister Marianna, and she was good to me. Then at the age of nine, my mother and her husband's life became complicated. Jesus lost his job and could not find work, and they were forced out from the home where we lived. I do not know what kind of work he did but it may have been in the construction business.

"Like I told you before, poverty can bring out the worst in people who otherwise may be good. Living without food and worrying about money often makes people angry. Then they behave poorly. My mother was angry at Jesus because they had no money. Marianna was always the independent and strong one, and she could walk away from unpleasant talks.

"Because of my mother's and Jesus' financial situation, my mother decided to take Marianna and me to Lima to live with our real father. I was nine, and Marianna was twelve. It affected Marianna more than me because she had always lived with our mother. I had only been with our mother for three years. But at least Marianna and I were together.

"At my father's, we lived in a two-bedroom apartment, and together in the apartment were my father's three children from a previous marriage before my mother—Robert, who was sixteen; Lucy, who was eighteen; and Celia, who was twenty years. My father had not remarried as my mother did. Now there was Marianna and me, and that made five children and my father. Robert had his own bedroom, and we four girls had the other larger bedroom. There was a very small room where my father slept. Mostly they all ignored Marianna and me and left us out of things they did.

"I went to primary school at Juana of Alarco Dammert in Miraflores in Lima. It was twelve blocks from my father's apartment, so I walked to school every day. It was a nice school, and I got along well with my classmates. I was a leader in my class, and sometimes I received diplomas for finishing a project or an assignment and helping the other students. Very early on, I began to like math very much and was good at it.

"School helped me to feel good about myself because the times at my father's and at my mother's before him were not happy. My father went to work at six o'clock in the morning, and we did not see him again until after eight o'clock at night. He worked at some paperwork job at the hospital nearby, I think. I do not remember what he did at the hospital. I do remember that I was sad. My father mostly ignored me when we were at the apartment. If I asked him for help with something, he said he was busy. I tried to be a good girl. I became sad and resentful. At the beginning, Marianna encouraged me to try to make the best of it. That was hard to do. I mostly concentrated on school because I liked it and it made me feel good. School kept me going because when I was learning, I felt content.

"I lived with my father for three years, and then he and my mother decided that I would do better if I lived with my Aunt Camilla, who was my father's sister. Camilla did not have children, and she had decided that she wanted to raise me as her own. She lived in Lima, and my parents agreed that it was the best solution. She was medium height, had made her hair blonde, and spent a lot of time on her looks and appearance. I was twelve, and I hoped that my life now would settle down and I could be happy and not so angry and confused. I moved into Aunt Camilla's house, which was even closer to school, and I was happy about that. Camilla was successful in her business as a clerk at a travel agency. Marianna went back to Arequipa to live with our mother who was now living with her husband. There Marianna finished high school. At first, Aunt Camilla was very excited to have me living with her, but soon she became moody, bossy, and possessive. I don't know what it was that made her angry; I think she had problems with her job and problems with her relationships.

"By this time, I thought that I was a bad person because everyone in my life had ignored me. People in my life did not ignore Marianna, so I thought she must be a better girl."

"Liz," I said, "it's insightful that you can understand this behavior after all these years. Look at the patterns. The behavior of your father, your aunt, and your mother, too, was never about you. You said yourself that these people were poor and hopeless. They ignored you because of their own frustrations and problems."

"Yes, dear Liz, I do know that now. It is common for some poor and unhappy people to treat their children this way. But that does not take away the pain of knowing that to a certain extent my family did not want me."

"I can tell you more," Liz went on. "I continued to go to school because it was an escape. By then, I was able to enroll in the El Vida Rodriguez secondary school in Lima, the one you call the junior high school or the middle school. I loved new subjects. Now I was interested in biology and even chemistry. Then, when I was fourteen and in the secondary school, my aunt Camilla's life and her work and her financial situation was getting complicated. She was frustrated and unpredictable. So I asked my mother if I could come back to Arequipa. I begged her. I mostly wanted to live with Marianna, who had graduated high school but still lived with Sofia and Jesus. Marianna was the only one who seemed to care about me, and I thought it would be good if I could spend more time with her.

"Finally my mother said okay. I moved to Arequipa and lived with my mother and her family and Marianna too, and that was the best part. I was depressed, and I buried that depression in school, where I continued to learn English. I would listen to any English television channels, and when I found a book in English, I would try to buy or borrow it. I had not yet had any training in English, but I planned to enroll for some when I finished high school. I was still interested in biology and chemistry, and more and more I thought about the dream in my heart, the dream to become a doctor. I never told anybody then because I thought they would tell me I was not realistic. How can a poor girl go to medical school without money or social position? I continued to learn English mostly in secret because no one else in my family was interested.

"During my final year of high school, my mother told me that I should study to become a hairdresser. She told me that I had to make a living for myself. I told her for the first time that I wanted to go to school to study medicine, and she said I should be realistic. I should become a hairdresser."

The hairdresser school was Sofia's plan for Liz. In spite of the distance between Liz and her mother, Liz obeyed. She went to hairdresser school as part of her last year of high school. After high school, she worked as a hairdresser. Liz hated the experience. It only brought her down more. And it put her on a path even further away from her dream.

# CHAPTER 6

# Standing Up

A typical school year in Peru begins in April and continues through December since, south of the equator, summer is January through March. Near the middle of November in 1989, only a month before Liz graduated from secondary school, the annual school dance was held. As in the United States, the event is hosted by the school for the students to socialize with their friends, play music, dance, and eat. The event took place at the school, and chaperones were selected for the event. A man named Carlos, the parent of a student in the class and a friend of several school families, was one of those chaperones. Carlos was a large man, more than six feet tall, with broad shoulders and black hair. He had the face of a man who had experienced many hardships and weathered them all. His eyes were deep set and dark, but they sparkled too and his smile was warm and genuine.

When it came time to pick the traditional godfather and godmother for the event, Carlos was easily chosen. A godmother was also selected, and together these two parents helped chaperone the event.

Carlos truly became a godfather to Liz, for what happened next was a peculiar set of events. A few weeks following the event, Liz was riding an Arequipa bus with her mother. Sofia was yelling at her before they got on the bus. She doesn't remember where they were going or why Sofia yelled. She says that today it doesn't matter. On the bus, Sofia was raising her voice at Liz, which caught the attention of others on the bus. Liz began to cry and was embarrassed. When the bus stopped, Liz stood up and got off the bus. She ran down the street—to where, she does not remember. She was sobbing and frightened, but at the same time, she felt free. She wandered down the street for what felt like a long time, with no destination in mind, with nowhere to go, but she was thinking, *I don't know what I will do, but I know I cannot go back to my mother.*

"When I caught my breath and looked around to where I was walking, I realized that I was very near to the home of Carlos, the kind man who was our event chaperone. I did not hesitate. I continued to walk but now with a destination in my mind. I knew that he would be kind and listen to me. I did not know anything else. I was frightened too. I was only sixteen, and I had no place to go. I had no money and nothing but the clothes and shoes I was wearing. I will never forget that day because, as alone as I was, I was determined to change my life. I was, as you say, pushed to my limit, and I made a decision that has changed my life."

From my conversations with Liz, it seems that Carlos, who knew many students and parents, was aware of Liz's home life. In any event, when Liz arrived at Carlos's home, she was visibly shaken. Carlos welcomed Liz into his home and into his family. Carlos had a wife and two daughters close to Liz's age. Liz did not know at the time that Carlos would become a dynamic force that would guide her through the years ahead.

"Carlos owned two small apartments in Arequipa in a building on Calle Samuel Velarde," Liz told me. "His elderly mother lived in one apartment on the first floor. He told me I could live in the other small apartment that was on the second floor. He said I could stay there for as long as I wanted. He gave me a bed and a few pieces of furniture and a bookcase. He has been my godfather ever since. I call him my uncle. He is not really my blood-related uncle, but dear Liz, he has been the unconditional love in my life since the day I got off the bus and left my mother. I do not know what I would have done without Carlos. He has welcomed me into his family like I belong there."

Liz continued, "My mother had insisted that I should be a hairdresser, and I learned how to do this during my last year of high school. I was a hairdresser and also studied English. When I was eighteen, I attended the Binational Peruvian American Cultural Institute for two years to study basic, intermediate, and advanced English. At the conclusion of these studies, I received a certificate of proficiency in English, and for the next two years I worked as an interpreter and as a tour guide. By then, I was twenty years old. I had some opportunities to work as an English interpreter for some companies that exported products like cameras, perfumes, and beauty products from Peru to Chile. The people at the companies were kind to me; they paid for all of my airfare and my expenses. This was the first time I was on an airplane. Also, during this time I worked as a tour guide, and it gave me great pleasure to show the wonderful things that my country has to share with the world. I also worked as an English teacher for parents who wanted their children to learn English. I had the certificate, so I could do this and I liked it. I was also able to work as a tutor to help children do better in their biology classes. I saved as much of the money as I could so I could pay for medical school."

In the United States, a person who is planning to attend medical school first studies a science such as biology or chemistry, graduates with a bachelor's degree, and then applies to medical school. In Peru, a person can attend medical school, and during the first two years completes biology and other sciences as part of the medical school experience. When the student graduates medical school as an MD, he or she is granted a bachelor's degree as well. So in Peru, the premed experience is considered part of Peruvian medical school. In both the United States and Peru, the next step is an internship.

In 1996, Liz was twenty-three years old, and with financial help from Carlos, she went to Lima for a year to study pharmacy at the University in Lima. "It was part of my plan," she told me, "to be able to take the entrance test for medical school at La Universidad Católica De Santa Maria, and the next year I took it and passed the test! My dream was going to come true! I could become the doctor like Juan Medina who helped me as a young child. But then, at the end of my first year, my uncle had very hard times with his work, so he could no longer help me. I had to drop out. I tutored English and taught biology again and tried to save money. But the tuition was so high that it was out of my reach. One semester of five months of class was 3,075 soles (US$1,050), and it was more than I could earn. I learned that the school would give me a loan through the bank, so the following year, in 1999, I applied for the loan and was accepted. I took another semester of medical school even though it has been a big break since the first year. Then I had to drop out again because I had to pay back the loan before I could get another loan."

Because the school required students to repay one loan before they could apply for another, a student like Liz didn't have a chance to get an entire loan for a college education. It seemed to me just another way to keep poor people from achieving a better life. When Liz showed me her classes and loan information, it appeared that the remaining balance on her school debt from 1999, including interest, was about 1,900 soles or US$633. Liz had paid off just $400 in four years. As I read the papers, I thought, *At this rate, if this young woman keeps starting and dropping out of medical school to pay off a loan each semester, she'll be an old woman by the time she completes school!*

"I was feeling hopeless with no way to fulfill my dream," Liz told me. "My uncle wanted to help, but he could not do much. Also, his health started to be bad, and he learned that he had a heart condition. In 2001, my uncle said I should be realistic. He encouraged me to go to the Federico Villarreal University in Lima to study education in the specialty of English as a second language. There are programs in my country that help students finish this kind of an education at very low costs, and it is not so expensive like medical school. During this time, I also worked as a secondary school teacher teaching chemistry and first aid to students." Liz said she had received certificates to teach these courses while she was in Lima studying pharmacy. By this time, which was February 2003, she had completed two semesters of medical school. But the school now told her that because of the strenuous demands of medical school, she could continue only if she became a full-time student. If that were not enough, she said the medical school had now changed the syllabus so that some of the classes she had taken earlier would have to be repeated.

During this time, while still living in Lima, Liz did some volunteer work with mission groups that came from the States such as our CSI group. This work gave her great satisfaction. In early 2004, she returned to Arequipa, hoping to be able to teach there.

"My uncle lives here now, so I can see him more and I can still stay in the room he has in the building where his mother lives. But I can only find part-time work and I still have the debt from the medical school, so I don't have much money even for food or the bus. But I do have Carlos.

He has been there for me ever since the day I got off the bus. He loves me. That is what I never had before."

"Liz," I said, "your story is amazing. To think that all these years you have stayed the course in spite of being poor and having no one in your life to help you or coach you until you found Carlos ..." I stopped.

"Yes, dear Liz, I know what you are thinking. In spite of my depression and sadness and having no money, I refused to believe that I couldn't do it. I would not take the drugs or the alcohol or become a prostitute. I would not do that because I believed in my heart and I still do that no matter how bad things are, I had to use my brain and try my best to live my life."

"And you know what else?" I said. "The day you got off the bus, *you stood up for yourself!*" I stood up from our table and pulled her shoulders to stand up across from me. I looked at her seriously and straight into her eyes. "Liz, that was the bravest thing you ever did. And it was the most important day of your life because you said, 'No more! I will not let anyone treat me poorly!' You stood up for yourself, and I am proud of you!"

We hugged. My heart ached as I heard her story, how Liz had been shuffled from family member to family member, each one discouraging her and bringing her down. How different my life has been, I thought, and how I took for granted the parents and the family I had, the encouragement and love I had received all my life. I never thought about that much until now. How was it that I was dealt a winning hand and Liz was dealt nothing?

On that day in December of 1989 when Liz got off that bus, she was frightened and scared but brave and proud. She found the strength to stand up, look forward and walk ahead. Liz did not see her mother for over five years.

# PART 2

Finding New Support

# CHAPTER 7

# Living Privileged

We can't always choose the cards we have been dealt, but
we can learn to play them.

—Smita Malhotra, MD

I grew up in Edina, Minnesota, one of the wealthiest suburbs not only
in the prosperous Twin Cities but also in the entire country. My father,
Clyde, was not born into wealth. He was the oldest of four children
raised by his mother, who supported the family as a seamstress in the
drapery department in Schunemann's Department Store in St. Paul. My
father's rise to leadership in an agrichemical business, Cargill, allowed
him to achieve, by age forty, the dream of a two-story stone-and-brick
Edina home with a sweeping yard and gardens. The house was set upon
a winding street with a promising name—Lakeview Drive. We lacked,
however, a view of the lake, a strange circumstance for my father, who
just then had found himself able to buy what he wanted. The lot he
first chose went straight down to the lakeshore, but in the week before
papers were signed, a tiny girl in a stroller, a girl scarcely younger than I
was at the time, managed to roll herself down to the water and drown.
In consequence, my parents retreated a block away from the dangerous
lake. However, we still lived on Lakeview Drive. Our family also owned
a summer home in northern Minnesota, two new cars every year, and
plenty of everything material that my older brother Mark and I needed
or wanted.

Both my parents grew up in the early 1900s and had humble

beginnings. Their parents, my grandparents, all migrated to America from various parts of Sweden in search of a better life than what Sweden offered at the turn of the century. They were sons and daughters of farmers with five or more children. The farms could not support the growth in the population, and there was not yet industry in the towns to employ the young people.

My father was smart and had some lucky breaks as a child. He found his way to a private secondary school and later to the University of Minnesota, graduating with honors in the school of business. He passed the CPA exam and worked first with the then PriceWaterHouse accounting firm. Later he attended the Harvard School of Business and moved on to become a senior executive with Cargill, from where he retired at age sixty-two.

What people who knew my father remember most was his ability to lead. He led every endeavor or interest he touched, as president of the Minnesota Cost Accountants, president of the Minnesota Christmas Tree Growers Association, and president of the University of Minnesota Masonic Cancer Hospital Fund, to name a few. He was a born leader and an outstanding public speaker. He could easily move people to join a cause he believed in. One of the qualities I admired about him most was that he used this talent for good and true purposes throughout his life.

Dad was the oldest of four children. His two sisters and one brother were wonderful as my and Mark's aunts and uncle throughout their lives. As an adult, I learned that Dad and his mother, Elizabeth, had been the victims of physical abuse by Dad's father and Elizabeth's husband, Oscar. Oscar was never in our lives, and legend has it that he was a heavy drinker and physically abused my grandmother. My father, being the oldest child, tried to stop the abuse and got in the way of Oscar's rage, thus also experiencing his abuse.

Like my father, my mother Elsie also grew up on St. Paul's east side, then a heavily Swedish community. She was an only child. Her parents, Ida and Magnus, were both from farming families in Stora Kopinge, Sweden. As life for farmers continued to be difficult, it was common to pursue immigration to America, where they dreamed of a better life and found it. Ida came to America when she was twenty-one, taking the sixteen-day journey by ship, and found her way to St. Paul, where she worked as an au pair and later as a seamstress. Magnus came to America five years later and worked as a farmhand on a steam-threshing machine in North Dakota. The following year, he found better pay working on the railroad and moved to St. Paul. Magnus and Ida had known one another in Sweden, and their relationship grew closer in St. Paul. They married in 1908.

My mother, Elsie, was born in 1909. Ida and Magnus were not wealthy, but their home was filled with laughter and time together reading and playing games. While Magnus worked for the railroad, they managed to save enough money to open their home as a boarding house. They rented rooms to local workers, and Ida provided home-cooked meals of all the popular Swedish dishes, including Swedish meatballs with lingonberries, lefse, rice pudding, Swedish pancakes, and traditional Swedish almond cakes.

Magnus took his young daughter Elsie to Como Park near their home to swing on the swing set for hours. Mother remembered that, when she was a child, he read and sang to her while she sat in his lap in the old rocking chair that was a main piece of furniture placed proudly in front of the fireplace. In 1918, Magnus contracted influenza and then pneumonia, and he died during the epidemic, leaving behind his devastated widow of forty-five and his nine-year-old daughter. From then on, Elsie and Ida were inseparable. Determined to care for her young daughter and continue the dream that she and Magnus had started, Ida became an entrepreneur of the times and her boarding-house business flourished. After school, Elsie helped with serving food and keeping the kitchen tidy.

After graduating from different high schools in St. Paul, my mother and father met at the Swedish Covenant church in their community, where the choirmaster put together an orchestra. Mother had taught herself to read music and play piano by ear, while Father studied violin. Their courtship lasted seven years, which was not uncommon during the Depression years. My mother completed high school, worked as a secretary for an insurance company in St. Paul, and devoted her life to the role of wife and mother.

The widow Ida lived with my parents after they married, also not uncommon in these times. Ida suffered a stroke in 1942 and died at the age of sixty-nine. My brother Mark was one year old. My mother expressed sadness that her mother did not live to meet me. She told me I reminded her of her mother and said we have many similar features. I've heard so many Ida stories that I feel like I know her. I have said that if I had a daughter, I would have named her Ida.

Mother remembered her father and talked about him, of course, through the eyes of a nine year old. I have often wondered what their lives must have been like. They had a mere ten years together before Magnus died, but Mother's memories of her parents and their life together are filled with love and kindness.

Their story is bittersweet for me. Growing up, I resigned myself to the fact that I had no relatives from my mother's family. After my father died of cancer at seventy-four, mother downsized from the big house on Lakeview Drive to an upscale apartment in St. Louis Park, Minnesota, just a mile away. When cleaning out the house on Lakeview prior to her move, mother and I found the old rocker, dusty and cracked, sitting in the attic as if it beckoned to be rocked.

"Oh, look, Liz, here's the old rocker. My father used to read to me and sing to me in this rocker!" she said, brushing the dust off with her hands. I saw in her eyes that, to her, it looked just as wonderful as it had when she was nine years old. "And now it is yours!" she exclaimed. "Along with the memories and the stories I've told you."

I had the old rocker restored, and now it sits beautifully in our great room. When I sit in it, I think about Magnus and Ida, poor immigrants who dreamed of a better life in America and found it, but then their good life together was cut short.

Like my new friend Liz in Peru, I too had hopes of becoming a doctor. I assigned all of my dolls illnesses that I could cure with my toy doctor set. Several of my first jobs as a high schooler were as a nurse's aide at local hospitals. It was at this time that I became serious about a career in medicine. The time was the sixties, and women more commonly became teachers or nurses. Although there were women physicians, the open doors for women in medicine were still a decade away. My parents encouraged me to become a nurse.

"After all," my mother said, "you'll be married one day, and your responsibility will be to care for your husband and your children. Being a nurse would be a wise and practical career choice for you."

I was close to my parents and trusted their judgment. Without any bitterness, I pursued nursing. It worked out well for me, and I went on to graduate school and had a satisfying and rewarding career. I always liked getting to know my patients and their families at a deeper level than I likely would have been able to do as a practicing physician. Still, I was not a physician.

In 1979, I accepted a position as director of nursing in California's San Gabriel Valley. I managed all aspects of the nursing and patient care areas of the hospital. While in Southern California, I finished a master's degree and a PhD in health care services, which opened many doors, and I thrived in my career. Also while in Southern California, I learned about a group of medical professionals who took weekend missions to remote areas of Mexico to provide clinic services. They were the Flying Samaritans, International. The Flying Sams, as they refer to themselves, is a nonsectarian, nonprofit volunteer organization of medical personnel, physicians, dentists, nurses, interpreters, and pilots who provide monthly medical and dental clinics in villages in rural Mexico at no cost to patients.. A friend had been on some of their weekend missions and shared with me what a great experience it was. She encouraged me to attend an informational meeting, and that was the beginning of some of the most rewarding experiences of my life.

Doctors, dentists, nurses, translators, pilots, and support personnel flew weekend missions to the clinics in Mexico in private aircraft. Through a cooperative agreement with the University of Baja California, the medical teams were sanctioned as "invited teachers." We flew out of Southern California early on a Saturday morning and arrived at our destinations in Baja, Mexico, by midmorning. Our aircrafts were four- and six-seater planes, piloted by wonderful Sams' pilots who donated their aircrafts and volunteered their time. Each mission included sixteen to twenty volunteer doctors, nurses, dentists, and interpreters. We all paid our own way for everything and shared the fuel cost. In addition, we solicited many items from the hospitals where we each worked. This might include surgical scrub attire that we would wear while performing procedures, a vast array of equipment that a hospital was ready to replace but was thrilled to donate to the Flying Sams, medications, syringes, bandages, and lab equipment. I recall one mission when our plane, a four-seater, had one seat occupied by a donated EKG machine; boxes of bandages and dressings; and a huge bag of tennis balls, stuffed animals, and toys for the children we would treat.

Landing on dirt runways in remote locations was common. On one mission, we were operating a clinic at Santa Ynez, a community on the east coast of Baja on the Gulf of California. As we were approaching the place where we would land, our pilot, Frank, let his passengers know we would be landing shortly. I looked out the window and saw fields, dirt, and tiny, flat-roofed houses. I could see we were very close to landing but saw no signs of an airport. I said in what must have been a rather weak and helpless voice, "Where … where … is the … airport … and the … runway?" Frank and the other two passengers laughed when Frank said, "No problem, Liz. It's right … *here*" as the wheels touched down on a partially cleared strip of dirt surrounded by field. This was my first lesson in mission improvisation! We figure out what needs to be done, and then we just do it.

When the plane stopped, I saw the three other planes in our group landing, and very soon, Mexican children and parents ran to us waving. Today the Flying Sams have ten chapters in California and Arizona and provide health care and education to more than seventeen villages in Mexico.

I've participated in medical service missions in multiple countries, mostly in Latin and South America. These experiences have opened my eyes to the harsh reality of poverty and overwhelming need in the world. I knew poverty existed in the United States, but growing up a privileged kid in an all-white community gave me no real exposure to the three billion people on the planet who live at or below poverty level all of their lives. As a young woman, having the opportunity of exposure to other cultures, conditions, diversity, and hardships that people throughout the world must endure every day of their lives has been the most valuable experience of my career. Medical service missions open eyes. They opened mine.

# CHAPTER 8

# Saying Goodbye

As the 2004 mission ended, we were exhausted. But at the same time we also felt a new surge of energy. Eighty-nine surgeries were completed, five more than first scheduled. There were no patient complications. Eighty-nine lives were changed.

During the previous seven days and into the evenings, I had listened to Liz Cardona's story of loneliness—her prison of sadness, as she called it. It made me ache inside. I couldn't help but think how opposite our childhood experiences had been. I was loved, supported, and encouraged and had opportunities. Liz had empty and unfulfilling parental relationships and had been without love or support from the people who were closest to her. While our lives were so very different, I felt a bond with her.

We both knew that in only a few days, I would be leaving Peru. Neither of us had raised the topic: Would we ever see each other again?

The surgeries were done, but there were still two symbolic events that needed to take place. It was traditional for the in-country hospital, doctors, and nurses to host an event to express appreciation to the American team for crossing borders to help the people of Arequipa. The event was scheduled for the hospital auditorium at two o'clock on the mission's last day.

The Peruvian chief of staff, chief of medical services, and chief nursing officer would formally thank us for helping their people and teaching the Peruvian doctors and nurses and give each of us a certificate of appreciation. Then the Americans would thank the Peruvians for their hospitality. Following, there would be an exchange of small gifts with our Peruvian counterparts. For the Peruvian nurses, I brought stethoscopes that I had purchased at a medical supply store at home and small flashlights that my company donated for making night rounds on patients. These are always wonderful events. For a few hours, cultures don't clash and our differences become insignificant.

The appreciation event required an interpreter. At a quarter to two, as about forty Peruvians and our team of thirty-two entered the auditorium, I heard Steve Fairbourne, our mission documentarian and photographer, ask, "Do we have an interpreter?" Steve spoke fluent Spanish, but he preferred to have a Peruvian who worked on the mission do the interpreting.

"Liz Cardona can do it," I said.

"That would be great. Is she here?"

"She'll be here any minute. She knows this starts at two o'clock. I'll check the front entrance of the hospital and try to find her."

"Great," Steve said.

I raced out of the auditorium and down a long corridor toward the hospital entrance. I felt my heart pounding by the time I reached the front door. Even after having been there for eight days, the altitude still made me short of breath.

I thought Liz would be coming by bus and hoped she wasn't delayed. I wanted her to do the interpreting. I wanted her be in front of the people she had helped all week and receive the thanks she deserved.

Just outside the front entrance, I saw Liz walking up the hospital's circular drive. "Hurry up, Liz!" I called as I ran to meet her. I don't know if I even said hello, but trying to catch my breath, I grabbed her arm and we began running together to the hospital entrance.

"The presentations are starting soon, and the American team wants *you* to be our interpreter. Let's go!"

"What? They want me to interpret for the doctors? Oh, dear Liz, I don't know if I can do that." Now she was getting out of breath too.

"What do you mean? Of course you can do it. You've been doing it all week! This is a great chance for you to show everyone how much you've helped us."

We raced down the hall. I am five foot two, and my husband kids that when he walks normally, I need to jog to keep up. Now I was walking rapidly, and Liz, at four feet ten, was jogging fast to keep up with me. I smiled, thinking I'd have to tell Tom I finally met someone who has to run to *my* walk! I slowed down.

"Catch your breath, Liz," I said as we entered the auditorium where people were standing in small groups chatting. Steve caught my eye and waved as Liz and I walked to him.

"Hi, Liz," Steve said as he put his arm gently on her shoulder and smiled. "We would so much appreciate if you would interpret for us. Are you okay with that?"

"Yes, I will be happy to do that," Liz said confidently.

"Wonderful. Come up here on the stage, and I'll show you where to stand. When the Peruvian doctors give their thank-yous," Steve said, "they'll stop every couple sentences so you can translate for your colleagues. Then you can do the same for us."

*Colleagues.* Did Liz hear that? He included Liz among Peruvian professionals.

As Steve and I began to leave the podium, Liz looked at me and said, "I am a little nervous, but I will do my best. I want you to be proud of me."

"I *am* proud of you, Liz," I replied. "Now be proud of yourself! You can do this. Be confident. Remember, no one else on the Peruvian team can do this!" I wanted to hug her but opted for professionalism. I squeezed her hand instead, and she squeezed mine.

As I took my seat, Liz straightened her lab coat and checked her lapel microphone. She was so short that she could barely see over the top of the podium. Realizing this, she stepped out to stand next to the podium so that she was in full view of the audience. "Good thinking, Liz!" I said to myself. Gazing down at the audience of nearly eighty people, Liz looked great—relaxed and not nervous. The audience quieted. Steve whispered in the ear of the Peruvian chief of staff, pointed to Liz, and said something in Spanish about Liz having helped us all week and being willing to do the interpreting. Then Steve stepped down from the stage and sat next to me.

As the program began, my mind wandered to Liz and our conversations. I had discovered this kind and sweet but unloved and unappreciated woman. She wasn't angry or hateful. Instead, she simply wanted to become a doctor. That was still somewhat difficult for me to understand, as was her acceptance of poverty. I guessed that when you have nothing, there is nothing to miss.

I was blessed with material possessions, anything I wanted or needed really. However, at this moment, none of that seemed important. I felt a deep gratitude for my upbringing, my husband, and the love I had throughout my life. At fifty-eight, I was learning something about myself.

Throughout the program, Liz interpreted beautifully. She stumbled a few times but recovered right away. The audience never noticed. The chief of staff acknowledged and thanked Liz for participating on the mission and interpreting. When the speeches ended, the chief of staff shook Liz's hand and put his arm around her, and I could tell he was saying something nice to her. Liz smiled. At the end, the applause was for the speakers, but Liz felt it too. I had a lump in my throat.

At that moment, Dottie looked at me, smiled, and said, "Liz did a great job, didn't she! I'm going to go up there and tell her!"

As I looked about the room, I saw Esmeralda, the hospital administrator, sitting with a group of Peruvian physicians. She scowled and I recalled one day when Liz and I were in the surgery area to transfer a patient to postop. Esmeralda was there as well. When she saw Liz, she yelled in Spanish, "What are you doing here? You are not allowed here!" Mary Jameson, one of our surgical nurses who spoke fluent Spanish, was nearby and said in Spanish, "Liz is translating for us. And she's doing a great job too!" as she winked at Liz and kept walking. Liz and I wheeled our patient's crib past Esmeralda and into the hallway without comment. I hadn't thought about the incident since. *I'll have to ask Liz what that was about*, I thought.

There was one more event, the mission dinner, which was hosted by the American team at El Camaroncito, a local restaurant. In addition to mutual thanks, the Peruvians would want to know if we would return the next year. That was a difficult question to answer since we could not make promises until the team had evaluated all aspects of this mission. Also, in addition to securing personal commitments, nearly $100,000 would need to be raised to cover air flights, hotels, transportation, and general mission expenses.

When we arrived at the restaurant, the Peruvian team invited us to join them at their tables. Norrie, Dottie, and I were given chocolates and beaded coin purses woven from alpaca. I still treasure the gift. Esmeralda, the hospital administrator, had compiled their guest list, and Liz wasn't included. I wondered why. What was going on? Since Esmeralda did not speak English, I asked Norrie to ask her why Liz wasn't invited. Norrie asked her and translated back to me: "Esmeralda said that Liz is not an employee of the hospital and only employees were included."

That wasn't true. A volunteer ophthalmologist, Dr. Carlos, who identified potential patients in Juliaca and accompanied them to Arequipa, was included. Also included were the families who freely housed parents of the Juliaca patients while they were in Arequipa.

"That's strange, don't you think, Norrie?" I said.

"I agree. Liz was a huge asset to this mission. I think Esmeralda is just using her power as the hospital administrator," said Norrie. "Don't worry. Liz is a tough girl who can take Esmeralda's disrespect."

The following day, a Sunday, we went to the hospital to pack up the equipment and supplies that would be air-freighted back to Minnesota. I had told Liz it would be our final time together, and it was the first time we talked about my leaving. Liz was at the hospital when we arrived. I could tell that she was sad, and I think I saw her crying as we taped and labeled boxes.

"Liz," I said, "I was disappointed that you were not at our dinner last evening. Do you know why Esmeralda didn't include you?"

"Well, yes, dear Liz, I do. When I learned about your mission, I went to see Esmeralda to ask if I could be a translator. Esmeralda yelled at me and said, 'They don't want you. They have enough interpreters! Go away and don't come back because this group doesn't need you!'"

"Oh, my, that's terrible. Why would she say that?" I asked.

Liz lowered her head, a sign that, I was learning, meant that she was sad or felt ashamed or inferior.

"You see, I am not of the Spanish descent. I am more native Peruvian. Esmeralda is Spanish Peruvian. She is quite white, like many of the doctors. There is class and race discrimination here. Esmeralda thinks I am inferior. It is nothing new; it is just the way it is."

"Well, discrimination isn't unique to Peru. We have plenty of it in the United States. We were all disappointed that you were excluded because you have been such an asset to our team."

"Thank you, but it is okay. I am used to it. I would not have been able to come because I did not have anything to wear and I would have to take the bus to that part of town, which is farther away and I did not have the coins I needed."

I felt sad and stupid for not having figured this out earlier.

The others who helped with packing were talking among themselves. I put my arm around Liz. She hugged me and cried. I knew that she wasn't crying because of the stupid dinner. She was crying because we were going to have to say goodbye. I felt the same way. I felt tears coming, but held them back.

"Liz," I said, "let's go down to the cafeteria and talk. We're done packing. I have twenty minutes before our taxis arrive."

It was ten o'clock in the morning, and the cafeteria was empty. We sat down, and Liz said, "Dear Liz, this has been an amazing week for me. I never thought that when I volunteered and received such a cold side, that I would find Mary Alice from your group, who made me feel so welcome and introduced me to you. You have been so kind to me, and you have let me tell you about my life. This has been a very low time for me. It has been painful to tell you everything. When I met you, it was like someone who cares to hear about me. It was like you were Juan Medina."

She was crying.

"Liz," I said, "this has been an incredible week for me too. I never thought I would meet such a person as you. Look at me. You *are* an amazing young woman. You have a beautiful heart, and you have a gift of compassion. I saw this in you every day this week. Every time you touched a child or a parent, every time you instructed the mothers, I saw the gifts you have." I squeezed her hands tight. "Growing up, Liz, you just never had a chance.

"I don't know what the future will hold for you or for us," I said, "but I will not forget you. I want to talk to my husband about some ideas I have. Let's exchange emails and telephone numbers and addresses. We'll stay in touch."

"Thank you, dear Liz. I would like that very much."

"Liz," I said, "I won't forget you."

We both stood up and hugged each other.

"Remember what I told you," I said. "You are capable of great things."

Then we walked together to the hospital driveway where our cabs waited. Liz was going to take the bus to her apartment. I realized that I had never gotten to see her apartment. I wondered what it was like.

I hailed our cab and waved to Liz. We blew kisses to each other. I got in the cab with two others on our team, sat back in my seat, and took a deep breath. As we drove away, I saw Liz walking to the bus stop, but she didn't see me. Now I had tears. *No, Liz, I won't forget you,* I thought. A pediatrician sitting next to me in the cab said, "Oh, there's Liz. You guys got to be pretty good friends, didn't you? Isn't that a coincidence, that you two have the same name? Maybe you were meant to meet here."

I responded with some pleasant agreement. He saw that I was being quiet and reached his hand out to my shoulder. "I'm glad you met her, Liz. We all know how much she liked you."

At the hotel, we packed our things and bused to the airport for our afternoon flight to Lima and then on to a night flight to Houston and finally on to Minneapolis.

Once on the airplane in Lima, I felt exhausted. We all did. The chatter we had heard on the flight down to Peru was silenced. Soon after takeoff, many of the team fell asleep. I was tired too, but I couldn't get Liz out of my mind.

I wondered if any of the people in Liz's early life—Etelvina, Sofia, Mateo, or Aunt Camilla—had loved her. She was ignored by all of these people. What was it that kept her going? Was it really Juan Medina? Did Marianna inspire her? Her uncle Carlos must have been a huge influence. I wished I had met him. There was so much I didn't know.

Then I had a sinking feeling. *Will I ever see her again? Get realistic! You are going back to Minnesota and a job you love.* Between our worlds, Liz's and my definitions of *normal* were a half a world apart. I felt sad. Then I said to myself, "I will see Liz again." She wants to be a doctor, and I am sure that she would be a wonderful physician! She is kind, caring, and gentle, and she's a good listener—although at the same time I had to admit that I didn't know many doctors in the United States who were great listeners.

Liz had volunteered her time that could have been used to tutor her students, when she would have made some money, but she loved being in the hospital setting with doctors, nurses, and patients. I think I realized why I had felt pulled to go to Peru. Is there such a thing as destiny? Were

Liz and I destined to meet each other? Somehow, I thought, between our worlds, I wanted to find a way to help this young woman realize her dream. I wondered if it was even realistic to be thinking about this. I knew there was a lot I did not know or understand, starting with the demands of medical school in Peru. But I was determined to try.

# CHAPTER 9

# Decisions

Upon returning home, it took a few days before I got back into the swing of my regular patterns. It always did. Following any mission, I felt somewhat unsettled. I had been gone two weeks, but I felt like I was still in Peru. I was grateful for the simplest things. In Peru, cabs are small and the roads in poor repair. Public toilets don't have seats. So I appreciated my comfortable though still small Mazda and my well-kept bathroom. We all referred to "getting used to life back home" as reentry to our regular lives.

The difference with my reentry from this mission was that I could not get Liz Cardona off my mind, nor did I want to. I was excited. I felt I had a project and a purpose.

Tom and I had spoken briefly while I was in Peru. He knew Liz was an interpreter for the mission, that I had learned a lot about her life, and that we had become friends. But I hadn't shared details of the "Liz story," as I was already calling it. Now, as I told him Liz's story of loneliness and ambition, I felt the same emotions come over me that I had felt in Peru. Then I said, "I want to give Liz the opportunity to study medicine. Tuition at the Catholic university where Liz is already accepted is 615 soles a month—or US$1,025 a semester. Two semesters a year would be about $2,050 a year. I can afford that. Can we talk about this? What do you think?"

There have been many times that I have been grateful for the open and honest partnership that Tom and I share in the dozen years we've been together. We look at the world in many of the same ways. Tom is an only child who grew up in a loving family. While his parents weren't poor, they did have childhood struggles and lived through the Great Depression, so Tom easily relates to people who go without what I always considered necessities. He has often offered work to someone who was in need or even just plain down and out. For years, rather than trading in a car, he sold them at a cheap price and on credit to people who needed transportation. When I asked him if he was afraid of being burned if the person didn't deliver on the agreement, he said, "Sure, it's a risk, but if someone reneges, then maybe he needed the money more than I did."

So Tom's response to my interest in helping Liz with medical school wasn't surprising. "I think it's a good idea," he said. "You never had kids to help, so here's your chance. It could be a good experience for both of you. And," he added, "it's not like you'll pay for everything at once. If it doesn't work out, stop."

Still, helping Liz was more than lending a hand or helping a person with car payments. If things went well, it would mean making a commitment for about six years. And I had questions. Medical school everywhere is challenging and demanding. Could she cut it?

In 1998 and 1999, with Carlos's help, Liz had completed two semesters of medical school. Then, in the middle of a semester in 1999, she had to quit school because of Carlos's health and financial problems. Her grades were mostly 10s and 12s on a scale of 9–20. Although far from exceptional, they were passing. But those two semesters occurred six years ago. Would being away from medical school for six years be a problem for reentering? Liz told me she was twenty-nine years old. Would her age be a problem? I knew from Liz that most of the students at the Catholic University of Santa Maria were from relatively wealthy families and were the sons and daughters of doctors, scientists, lawyers, business owners, and other professionals. How would Liz's culture of poverty and appearance as a more native Peruvian play out at such a place?

Completion of a medical degree in the United States involves four years of premed and then medical school, an internship, and residency. In Peru, I soon learned, the commitment to become a doctor required three years of basic medical study, three years of clinical work in the hospitals, one year as an intern, and a year as a resident, known as the SERUMS. During the internship, students continue to study and complete a thesis.

Successful completion of these seven years through the internship ended in the award of a bachelor's degree and an MD degree. Then an additional year had to be spent in the SERUMS, a national program that places newly graduated MDs in underserved rural communities throughout Peru for ten months to practice medicine. Importantly, completion of SERUMS is required in order for a physician to be admitted to practice in Peru's public hospitals. Following the SERUMS would also be a residency program for those who wished to specialize in a particular field. I would learn over the coming years that the demands, expectations, stress level, and medical student issues in Peru were quite similar to those that US medical students report.

Tom and I talked about the possibilities for Liz's success and her potential for failure. Was I prepared to lose the money I would give Liz for medical school if she didn't finish? I thought about the money Tom and I gave to charities. As donors, we can read reports from organizations to gain some confidence about how our gifts are used, but that's usually the best we can expect. If I give money to Liz, I thought, at least I will know exactly where it's going. If she doesn't succeed, I will know I tried. I found some satisfaction in this. In any case, charitable money spent is gone whatever the cause—personal or institutional. The difference here would simply be that because the money went to Liz personally, I'd get no tax deduction.

I also knew I had an emotional commitment as well. Never having had children, I found myself, at age fifty-eight, feeling and behaving the way my parenting friends felt about their college-age sons and daughters. At this point, I didn't consider Liz an adopted daughter, but I knew I had a passion to help her overcome poverty. How would I feel if she failed, couldn't make the grades, dropped out, changed her mind, or, worse, wasn't the person I thought she was when we bonded in Arequipa? Was I prepared for the many not-so-positive outcomes and disappointments? To these questions, Tom reminded me that these are the risks of being a parent. Things don't always turn out the way you imagine.

What if my hopes for Liz's finishing medical school, practicing as a physician in Peru, and helping people in poverty didn't turn out the way we thought it would? Could I handle that? I decided I could, but at the same time I was determined to make it work for Liz. *Liz will do this,* I thought. *She wants it too much to fail!*

I'm an optimist, maybe to a fault. In my relationship with Liz, I knew I had to be one. Liz had never had the opportunities that the children of parents I knew had, yet her goals and expectations for herself were greater than any American kid I knew.

I knew that if this were going to work, I would also need to be a coach, a mentor, and yes, a parent since Liz had no parental support except for Carlos. I knew I had to be positive. I knew that she would not want to let me down. I thought of the cliché we are tempted to say when we hear this: "But, Liz, you'd only be letting yourself down." I believed that Liz would not let herself down. Except for Carlos, adults in Liz's life had let her down, yet she seemed to know at a very young age that she had a purpose, and if given the opportunity, nothing would stop her from succeeding. This was a journey of which I wanted to be a part.

A few days later, I decided to call Liz to tell her again how much it meant to have her on our mission. By now we were good friends. She beat me to the phone call. She was at an internet café.

"Dear Liz," she said. "I wanted to hear your voice. How are you doing, dear Liz? Are you rested after your journey back to the US?"

First, we exchanged small talk about my trip home. I asked her about Arequipa and what she had been doing since the mission ended. She had continued to tutor some students and was looking for a steady job in order to pay off her school debt. We both said we missed our long talks over *saltado* and Inca Kola. She sounded happy. I missed her.

"Liz," I said, "when we were together in Peru, you told me that the university would not give you your grades until you paid off your loan. What is that amount?"

"The university says I owe 1870 soles. I am continuing to do the tutoring so I can continue to pay the debt."

"Well, I know you're working hard to pay this debt, but Tom and I have talked and decided that we will pay it. What is the amount you would need to pay for your next semester in medical school? I will send you the money. Then you will be able to get your grades and move on."

"But for the entire semester, it will be $205 a month or $1,025 for the semester."

There was a long pause. "Liz? Are you there Liz?" I said.

I could hear her. "Liz, are you okay?" I asked.

"Yes, dear Liz, I am fine. I am overcome with the joy I feel. When you were here in Peru and we had the long talks into the evening, I felt like someone had come into my life and come into my heart. I never had that before. That was a joy enough, for me to know that you were thinking of me and we could write and talk sometimes on the phone calls. Now I hear what you say to me and I am thanking God …"

I think I interrupted her. "I know, Liz, and I'm glad we met too, and I'm happy that I can help you. Now you need to send me your bank information. The name of your bank, the account number …"

I stopped. *Did she even have a bank account?*

"Liz, do you have a bank account?"

"No, dear Liz, I do not."

"Ok, well, you need one. Go to a bank that you or your uncle know and open an account. Can Carlos help you with that?"

"Yes, he will. He has an account at the Interbank here in Arequipa. I'll go there."

"Then you need to send me the bank name and address and your account number and the bank swift code number for international transfers. Do you understand?" I asked.

"Yes. I will do it, dear Liz."

"Okay, that's good. Then I'll wire the money you owe. Then, I want you to tell me what the cost of the total tuition is for the next semester. I want you to get back into medical school."

I paused. I had a lump in my throat and tears in my eyes. Was I feeling sorry for Liz? Did I love this girl as if she were my daughter? I don't know. I didn't know what loving a child felt like.

There was another silence on the phone, but I knew we hadn't been disconnected. Then I heard her crying softly.

"I … don't know what to say. I cannot think of words," she finally said.

"Well, I'll talk then. It was a special thing that we met in Arequipa. I believe that people come into each other's lives for a reason. You said when we met it was a very low time for you. So maybe it was meant for us to find each other. We are two Elizabeths who met on that beautiful day in Arequipa. Maybe you needed to meet me, to have me in your life. And maybe … I needed to find you too," I said.

"Well, dear Liz, I too believe that God brings people together for a reason, for a purpose. I could feel it when we met that we had a bond with each other right from that first day Mrs. Mary Alice introduced us. You were so easy to talk to, and you were so kind to me. But I only hoped to have you in my heart in emails and perhaps some talks through the telephone."

"Well, now we will have a project together. You'll be doing the hard part, going to class and passing the tests. I'll pay your tuition. Now you need to send me the amount of tuition for the next semester that will be starting in August."

"Yes, I will do that. But, Mamita—may I call you Mamita? It is a term of endearment in my country. My heart is so full of thanks for what you are doing for me. You are like an angel. I am very emotional. Please forgive me."

"Liz, that's fine, and I understand. We had many emotional conversations when we were together in Peru. I know how difficult it was for you to talk about your childhood and the loneliness you felt growing up. But Liz, Tom and I believe that you can finish medical school because you are brave and determined. Think about how you have persevered to continue your studies. Now I will help you get through these years in medical school. We know you can do it."

"I won't let you down, Mamita. I will make you proud of me."

"I am already proud of you, Liz. Now you be proud of yourself. You will succeed. We will succeed together. Now email me the information I need, and we'll talk again soon. I will call you next time. Don't spend money on phone calls."

"I understand, Mamita. I love you, dear Liz."

"I love you too, Liz."

I hung up. I sat at my desk in my home office and cried. I wasn't sad; I was overcome with a full heart. I could help make Liz's dream come to life, and I couldn't think of anything that I wanted to do more.

Liz and I continued to exchange emails and occasionally telephone calls. I learned I could buy a phone card at Walgreens specifically for calling to Peru at discounted rates. That helped.

By email, I learned that tuition for the semester starting in August was $1,025. I wired $1,077 into Liz's new bank account, an extra $52 as I learned there was a bank fee on Liz's end. No surprise there. As promised, Liz let me know two days later that the money was in her account. I set up a transfer account with our investment firm so that I could wire money to Liz with a simple phone call. It took three minutes. It was easy. I learned that if I wired from my account by eleven o'clock, it would reach Liz's bank the following day. Swift numbers, international transactions—I was learning a lot these days!

Soon, Liz enrolled at the university to finish the first semester of her second year. Her emails were filled with newsy academic discussions. She had quizzes every week in genetics and molecular biology and labs to complete in microbiology and pathology. She continued to tutor three young girls in biology and English three hours each weekend, for which their parents paid Liz thirty soles, or $10. I was learning about salaries in Peru too. An average nonprofessional person could expect to make five hundred to seven hundred soles a month, or about $166 to $233. The starting salary for a physician or an attorney was and is typically just $500 to $666 a month. I would later learn that there are various levels of pay for physicians. At the top, the chief of a specialty service or chief of staff of a hospital earns as much as $3,500 a month. It's not so much, but I knew a potentially high salary wasn't motivating Liz.

In a telephone conversation, Liz told me that the university registrar told her that because the university had changed the medical core syllabus, she would have to repeat some classes and would have to wait another year to enroll as a full-time student. "Why do I have this obstacle? I can't believe it."

Then she said, "I went to Lima last weekend to see my father." The trip from Arequipa to Lima is a twelve-hour bus ride each way, so it took a day to travel. Liz explained to her father what Tom and I were doing for her and asked if he could help her. He said he couldn't help because he was planning to retire and hopefully receive a pension. Liz said she understood his reasons.

"Now that I am back in Arequipa," she added, "I will look for some tutor jobs full time so I can save to cover the classes that I must repeat."

As I thought about it, I wasn't surprised that Liz would be required to repeat some classes before enrolling as a full-time student, nor was it surprising that Mateo had again been unable or unwilling to help. Carlos was willing to help but unable to do much. This turn of events presaged what lay ahead.

I interrupted her. "Liz," I said, "let's not let this be a problem. It doesn't have to be. Can you make up or repeat some of the classes during the August-to-December semester and then attend the summer session from January to March?"

"I think so, but it means more tuition and I—"

"You need to go to the registration or to a counselor at the university. Register for the classes you need to repeat. Try to fit them in over this August semester and in summer school. I'll pay for it. I told you I would help you with *all* of your medical school."

"But you have done so much already."

"Liz," I said, "we *want* to help you with medical school. I'm committed to this. Concentrate on your classes. When that time comes, tell me the cost and I'll wire it to you. Do you understand, dear Liz?"

"Yes, yes, I do. I am so grateful that I do not know how to speak it. I will talk to the university tomorrow, and I will send you the new curriculum and let you know the classes I am taking."

"That sounds great, Liz. Now don't worry about this. We're a team. You do the studying, and I'll make the payments."

"Yes, Mamita, we are a team. I love you for what you are giving to me from your heart."

As I told her that I loved her also, I thought of Mrs. Huahuamello again. Like her, Liz had nothing to give me but love. That was enough.

# CHAPTER 10

# Visitor Visa

Summer in Minnesota raced by. August was hot and humid, but in Arequipa, Liz told us, winter temperatures fell to twenty above zero or colder. Snow rarely fell in the city but often covered the three volcanic mountains surrounding it. Liz and I talked weekly and exchanged emails regularly. Tom figured out how to instant message with Liz, and the three of us had many conversations online. We talked about medical school, of course, but Liz also talked about Carlos, her sister Marianna, and the demonstrations that occurred prior to an upcoming political election. She sent a syllabus for the August semester and by early November had met with her adviser to lay out a curriculum plan. "This is my dream, Mamita," she said. "I am living my dream!"

As planned, she took the repeat credits during the August–December semester and registered for summer school from January to March in order to catch up with the rest of the classes. I was impressed but not surprised by her commitment. Liz was a few years older than most of the students in her class, and I wondered about her social life. Did she have one? Did she have a boyfriend? It was a topic we had not discussed when I was in Peru. I was curious and decided to ask her.

"I have had some boyfriends, but mostly they were good friends and not of the romantic kind. I have been so busy working and finding ways to go to school that I have no time for boyfriends," Liz said.

"Do you have girlfriends that you do things with? Certainly you have to do something for fun," I said.

"Yes, I have several friends who go to the university also. They are ahead of my class. We go out to a restaurant sometimes. And sometimes Marianna goes with us," Liz replied.

In late October, I asked again if she had met men in medical school. She said that yes, she had, but they were good friends and that several men and women had a study group together. "I am committed to my dream, to our goal, Mamita," she said. "Love can wait." I was glad she didn't have a love interest. She had a lot on her plate.

Tom and I talked about bringing Liz to Minnesota following her final exams in order to spend the holidays with us before starting summer school in January.

"I know there is such a thing as a visitor visa," I said to Tom. "Wouldn't it be good if Liz could visit us for the holidays?"

After looking into it, Tom learned that the Department of State granted visitor visas under certain circumstances and for short periods. We talked with Liz, and she was ecstatic at the idea and also researched the visa process. First, she would need to go to the US Embassy in Lima and request an appointment for a later date to present the visitor visa paperwork to the Consul General. The required paperwork included an application, Liz's passport, an application fee, and "convincing supporting documents."

We learned that the US immigration law presumes that applicants for nonimmigrant visas are intending to immigrate to the United States unless they can prove that they have family, property, business, or economic ties to Peru or other reasons to support that they have no intention of remaining illegally in the States.

Liz assembled her university admission papers, and two of her professors wrote letters stating that she was a full-time medical student. She had parents in Peru but no job and little real income, and she owned no property.

As a visitor's host, I was required to write to the US Embassy in Lima introducing us, giving our credentials, telling how we knew Liz, and providing a statement to assure them that Liz would stay at our residence and would return to Peru on a specific date.

Although cumbersome, the process seemed straightforward. We thought our letter covered everything without saying, "Do you think we would be stupid enough to risk going to prison for harboring an illegal immigrant?" It was a long shot, Tom guessed, but it would be great fun if Liz could spend the holidays with us.

Her second embassy meeting was several weeks away. At my request, Liz attached in her emails all the required paperwork, including a copy of her passport. I hadn't paid much attention, but when I looked at her passport copy, I noticed that her date of birth was February 18, 1973.

Hadn't she said she was twenty-nine when I met her this past May? I wondered. Her date of birth on her passport would make her thirty-one. I must have remembered her age incorrectly.

It wasn't a big deal, but I did mention it in an email. The next day I received a sorrowful email:

> Dear Mamita, It is true, I am not the twenty-nine. I said that because I felt shame for you to know that at this time in my life I am still studying. I am from 1973. I am thirty-one years, but the reality is that I have not accomplished anything and to be of this age is embarrassing when I have no career. Please forgive me. I am conscious that I will deserve a punishment for saying the wrong thing to you.

I sat back and read her words again. How did she think I would punish her for telling me her wrong age? People lie about their age all the time. When we talked about her age, we hardly knew each other, and she probably thought she'd never see me again. Nevertheless, there we were, a part of each other's lives. I didn't care about her age, but I did want her to understand that I now expected truthfulness as long as I was paying her tuition.

I called her. "Liz, it's me, Liz in Minnesota. Are you there?"

"Yes, I am here. I am so glad to hear you."

"I got your email—where you explained your age," I said.

"Yes, Mamita, I am ashamed. Please forgive me. I will not lie to you again, I promise to you. You are doing so much for me that I am filled with shame."

Time for an interruption. "Liz, I understand." Then I laughed as I recalled a story. "Actually, my previous husband lied about his age his whole life! And he changed his age on so many documents that I think he actually *did* get into some difficulty at one point." I was laughing aloud as I told Liz the story. She didn't get it. It was one of those stories that just wasn't funny across cultures. I got back on topic.

"Liz, I'm not upset. And I understand how you felt. You had just met me. And during our time in Arequipa, you were surrounded by doctors and nurses, some near your age, and you may have felt overwhelmed."

"Yes, I did. I felt that I had nothing to offer."

"That's silly. We couldn't have communicated with our patients if you hadn't translated. We all bring different skills and talents to a situation. So now tell me the truth always, and let's focus on the future."

We talked about her upcoming visa interview, and I tried to coach her on what to wear and say. She had no experience with this type of interview. The more I learned about the United States' tight control on immigration since 9/11, the more I doubted that she could pull it off. I doubted the US Embassy would say, "Well, here's a Peruvian doctor of tomorrow! Let's give her this visiting visa so she can see her new friends in the United States. She'll *certainly* want to return to her life of poverty in Arequipa!" Still Tom and I hoped. We wanted to see her.

November 8 came, and Liz, Tom, and I agreed that she would call us with the outcome of her interview. I was at work when Liz called Tom to say that her request had been denied. Tom called me. Liz had been upset on the phone, saying that the woman at the Consul General office was cold and fired off only three questions:

"How old are you?"

"I am thirty-one years."

"Are you studying?"

"Yes, I am a full-time medical student."

"Have you ever interrupted your studies?"

"Yes, two times, because I ..."

"I'm sorry, but your application will not proceed further. Denied. Next!"

While we were disappointed, I decided to contact Minnesota senators Norm Coleman and Mark Dayton, as well as Jim Ramstad, our representative. In emails, I explained that we were supporting Liz in medical school and wanted her to come to the United States on a visitor's visa to spend the holidays with us and return to Peru to start her summer school program. Within a week, Senator Coleman's office wrote to the US Embassy in Lima requesting reconsideration for granting the visiting visa for Liz. The letter stated that Liz had "essential ties" to Peru where she was a full-time student, that she had a teaching job, and that her family resided in Peru. It didn't mention that her "family" was absent in her life. Senator Coleman's office received a prompt response from the embassy saying that the presumption in US immigration law is that every visitor applicant is intending to emigrate. Applicants can overcome this presumption by demonstrating compelling professional, financial, and social ties to their home country. The communication went on to say that Liz's documents stated that she was a full-time student and did not have an income. In addition, she had taken time off from her university studies several times and still needed five and a half years of study to complete a degree. Thus, Liz could not prove to the consular officer that her ties to Peru were stronger than her ties to the United States.

Everything that the Consular General office said was true. In the eyes of the US Embassy, Liz was a poor risk in spite of our assurances. If Liz had lived in France or Germany, the outcome might well have been different.

We were all disappointed. "But Liz," I said, "we'll see each other again. Maybe on another mission or maybe Tom and I can visit Peru. Don't be sad. Focus on school."

Final exams for this first semester took place the week before Christmas, and she felt prepared. In addition, that same week, Liz emailed me that a fellow passenger had stolen her cell phone out of her bag while she was riding the bus home from school. I learned that there was no class distinction for stealing. Poor people stole from poor people as well as from the rich. Carlos remained in Lima where he continued to work in a bank, so Liz planned to spend Christmas alone in Arequipa, drinking hot chocolate while reading medical books. I called her late one evening.

"Would you like to go to Lima to spend the holiday with Carlos?" I asked.

"Oh, yes, Mamita, I would like to do that very much."

I wired money to Liz for a cell phone and a flight to Lima. On New Year's Eve, Liz sent an email from Lima:

This is the time for me to reflect on what this year has meant to me. I cannot begin to say how my life has changed since I have gotten back to my study. When I met you, I was sick in my soul because my life was so lonely. Now I have a new hope in my heart. I can see the future and it looks bright and happy. I thank you for allowing me to be a part of your life and for giving me this opportunity to study what has been my dream since I was a young girl. It is a miracle to me dear Liz. Someday, somehow, I will help a person in need as you are helping me. Happy New Year to you and Mr. Tom and please know that I love you with all my heart.

It was a good way to welcome in 2005.

# CHAPTER 11

# Etelvina

In January, Liz received her semester grades. They were mostly 11s and 12s, about a C+ in American universities. Although I wasn't disappointed, I knew she could do better. After all, I told myself, she'd been out of school for several semesters.

As the summer session began, Liz's grandmother, Etelvina, now eighty-five, was diagnosed with kidney cancer. She now lived in Lima with Aurelio and their daughter Camilla, Liz's aunt. Etelvina had raised Liz for six years, and while she had unhappy memories, Liz still thought of Etelvina as her early mother. "At first, she had abdominal pain," Liz informed me. "Then they performed a biopsy, and the doctors found the cancer. We hoped that she could have chemotherapy, but it has already spread."

Etelvina received opiates and was sent home. The health care benefits of one of her sons, a Peruvian marine, were extended to his mother. That helped with expenses. Etelvina's condition soon worsened, and Liz again took the twelve-hour bus trip to Lima to visit her. "She was suffering a great deal because there was no cure," Liz told me. "All of the family was waiting for the call of God."

Etelvina had a strong influence over Liz's aunt Camilla. She had tried to manage Liz's life as a young girl, telling Camilla how Liz should be raised. During our telephone conversation, Liz said, "My mama Etelvina and I stayed close until I was about twelve when I was living with Aunt Camilla. Then it wasn't so good."

"What happened when you saw Etelvina?" I asked.

"We said many things. I think we both want to be at peace. She said I looked beautiful and called me Rosie because my middle name is Rosita. She said, 'I am happy for you and so proud of you that you are studying to be a doctor.' Then she told me, 'Please forgive me, Rosie, for all the things I have done to you. I was wrong about so much.' We cried together and forgave each other for our mistakes. It was everything to me for her to say after all these years she is proud of me."

A few days later, Etelvina died. Her eight children bought a coffin and a cemetery lot in Lima. A Catholic funeral was held. Etelvina was buried below the ground. Liz told me that they said it was a beautiful place, green and private.

"How did Sofia handle her mother's illness and death?" I asked Liz in a phone call.

"I did not see my mother in Lima, and I was not able to be at the funeral because of school. Everyone was sad, and she was too, I suppose. But you know, I have not been close to Sofia, so I did not have a conversation or any talks about it with her because we are not that way."

Aurelio was still independent. He was in his late eighties and worked part-time in sales. Liz didn't see him often because she had little time to go to Lima. If he came to Arequipa, he sometimes tried to see Liz. "I can't do anything to help him because I have no income," she told me. "I wish I could, but I can't until I finish school. I love him because, like my grandmother, I grew up with him and knew him as my father."

In summer school, Liz took biostatistics, biophysics, and Microbiology II for eleven credits. I thought this was a heavy schedule for a ten-week semester, but Liz said she could manage. Upon completion of these classes, she could enroll as a second-year medical student in March. She was happy and upbeat. In January, she wrote:

> I am filled with excitement to be in school and studying what I have wanted to do all of my life. I am convinced of myself, that I will complete the studies to become a doctor. I look forward with hope and confidence to give a better quality of life to the patients I will care for one day.

# PART 3

## Goals Conflict with Memories

# CHAPTER 12

# Mission 2: Return to Arequipa

In March 2005, Liz enrolled for the next semester. Taking a heavy load the year before and summer school classes paid off. She was now recognized as a second-year medical student and registered for microanatomy, Biophysics II, Biostatistics II, molecular biology, and another microbiology class. It was a challenging schedule, but Liz assured me that she was up for it. I was thrilled to hear the excitement in her voice as she spoke about her classes.

"I am in a study group with ten students, Mamita. We are all taking microanatomy. We work together in class and study the different parts of the human brain. Last week we decided to purchase another brain for our studies. It will be a better example."

"I'm glad you and your colleagues are getting a better brain." I laughed. "How much does a good brain cost in Peru these days?"

"It will cost about six hundred soles, or two hundred dollars," she said.

*How stupid of me,* I thought. It hadn't dawned on me that Liz would have to buy books and supplies. When she started working in the hospital and seeing patients, she would need a stethoscope and scrubs and more supplies as well.

"Please email me the cost of books and supplies," I told her. "And, Liz, I'll send extra for your share of the *better* brain."

Early in 2005, CSI held a team meeting to evaluate the last mission and plan an Arequipa mission for June 2005. Tom attended with me.

The team reminisced about our 2004 experiences and looked at pictures of the hospital, patients, and the procedures. Afterward, the board and the mission coordinators put together a team of doctors, nurses, medical equipment specialists, medical records specialists, and a logistics coordinator who would lead the new mission. I agreed to participate, again in the preop/postop nursing role. Tom volunteered for medical records, which didn't require medical expertise but did demand organizational skills. He teamed with Mary Lou, a volunteer who spoke fluent Spanish. Now all we needed to do was raise $100,000.

I called Liz. "Guess what? CSI is working to raise money to come to Arequipa again in June, like last year. And Tom will be on the team."

"Oh, Mamita, I am so happy to hear this incredible news!" she replied. "To think we will see each other again in a few months. I have prayed for this to happen. And to meet Mr. Tom will be wonderful too."

Liz didn't know how excited Tom and I were to be able to participate in another mission. I loved what our team had done in Arequipa, and now we were going to do it again. Knowing that I would see Liz and that Tom would meet her made my heart pound. Liz's dream to become a doctor was coming true, and I shared in her dream as well.

### Raising Money

We organized a fund-raising event with Canterbury Downs, a racetrack near Minneapolis. A portion of weekend proceeds from entrance fees went to CSI, and we held a silent auction there as well. Businesses and individuals donated items ranging from dance lessons to pieces of art, and horse racing fans bid on the items. To my amazement, CSI made more than $20,000 that day.

Volunteers also organized a fund-raising gala at the Mill City Museum in Minneapolis. Again, we held a silent auction, and many of us who had participated on missions with CSI donated items. Tickets for the dinner were $125 per person. Tom and I invited five couples to attend. We heard back from three couples—my brother Mark and his wife, Jackie, and two other couples who knew about the 2004 mission and our commitment to Liz Cardona. With our friends' and our own donations, we raised $1,000, and the event netted more than $60,000. With $80,000 in hand, it looked like the mission would happen.

At that time, I worked in compliance at the corporate headquarters in Minneapolis for Ceridian Corporation, a large international company that provided technology, payroll, and human resource services. Ceridian had a Lunch and Learn program. Any employee who worked with a community group, charity, or special cause could invite employees to bring their lunches and attend a noon-hour presentation that took place in a conference suite. This, at Ceridian, was an important legacy from its earlier years as Control Data Corporation, a company very committed to community improvement.

Mike Fairbourne, a CSI board member and a well-known and well-liked television meteorologist in the Twin Cities, and I created a Lunch and Learn presentation showing the 2004 mission, including dramatic before and after surgical pictures. Attendance was good and interest high. Highlights of our presentation appeared in Ceridian's monthly newsletter that was distributed to all locations. Over the weeks that followed, I received contributions for CSI from Ceridian employees all over the country. Some employees sent checks in amounts of $20 to $50 with warm, heartfelt notes. Others went to buy Children's Tylenol, thermometers, bandages, notepads, and toys for the kids. Soon, my office was filled with boxes of donations for our June mission. I was thrilled at the interest and generosity from my colleagues. Ceridian also gave CSI $500 through a community-outreach program where employees could apply for a corporate donation for a nonprofit organization where the employee volunteered.

CSI also negotiated a discounted airfare for our team of thirty-one to fly Continental Airlines to Lima and a discount from the Casa Andina Hotel in Arequipa. The hotel was happy to do it. We were helping their people, and we filled nearly half their rooms.

CSI told each mission participant that we were expected to raise or write a check for $700 to help cover airfare and hotel costs. CSI told me, however, that since Tom and I had already raised more than $1,700 from the dinner, Ceridian, and its employees, our obligation was fulfilled. But Tom had spent twenty years in development and fund-raising and felt strongly that gifts received from other people should not be considered a personal donation. I agreed. We wrote our check.

As the mission neared, CSI asked us if we would travel with a small group of doctors, nurses, and a translator to help screen potential patients in Juliaca, a remote city located high in the Andes where there was a high incidence of children with cleft lips and palates. Because the language spoken in this part of Peru was Quechua, or a mixture of it and Spanish, we thought Liz would be a big help there. When CSI balked at paying the $180 airline fare for Liz to fly with our group to Juliaca, I called Mary Batinich, our 2004 mission coordinator, who was on CSI's board.

"Mary, you remember Liz from last year," I said. "She is volunteering again as a translator, and she is willing to help us in Juliaca. Did you know that Liz is also fluent in Quechua? I understand that CSI does not want to pay for her airfare. If this is a money issue, Tom and I will pay for Liz's ticket." The next day, the board agreed that Liz should go to Juliaca and that CSI would pay her airfare.

Liz, Tom, and I had many phone conversations and emails. We were excited. Liz wanted to show us the university and introduce us to Carlos. I also intended to see her apartment, something I had wanted to do the previous year but there was no time.

On a Thursday afternoon in June 2005, thirty-one of us—some old friends from last year and some new faces—left Minneapolis for Newark and boarded Continental's night flight to Lima. In Lima, we proceeded through lengthy but uneventful customs inspections and a several-hour layover before we boarded a Lan Peru flight to Arequipa. I sat in a window seat with my nose on the acrylic, looking down in awe of the jagged mountain peaks and thinking about my last trip. I had tears in my eyes as I thought of how far we had come. Liz had been in medical school full-time for an entire year. We had a long way to go, but I looked forward with enthusiasm. The Andes mountains seemed to have no beginning or end for they were all I could see. I thought that maybe it was like Liz and me.

# CHAPTER 13

# A Mission Almost Aborted

Although our surgeons often carried personal instruments and equipment with them, CSI owned other equipment, specifically anesthesia gear. Getting that equipment to Peru, through its customs, and delivered to Arequipa ahead of our arrival was the responsibility of our logistics coordinator, George, a retired US Army lieutenant general who was proud of his organizational skills. He served on CSI's board of directors and wanted to go to Peru but spoke no Spanish.

During the flight from Lima to Arequipa, George and two doctors—Xavier, an anesthesiologist fluent in Spanish, and Dick, a plastic surgeon who headed the medical team—questioned whether the equipment had arrived at the hospital in Arequipa because George had not received a confirmation of arrival from Honorario Delgado Hospital before leaving Minneapolis.

Late Friday morning, we arrived in Arequipa. When I stepped off the plane, once again I felt the familiar light-headedness of the eight-thousand-feet altitude but knew it wouldn't last long. There were no Jetways at the small airport, so we disembarked down the rolled-up stairway. Immediately, I saw Liz waving to me from the airport passenger waiting room. I was so excited to see her that I ran ahead of everyone else.

"Mamita! Mamita!" Liz screamed as we hugged each other hard. Tom needed no introduction. He and Liz hugged too. Hugs, tears, and introductions to the others on our flight followed. We retrieved our luggage and headed for our bus, and Liz joined us for the ride into the city. On the bus, I put my arm around Liz's shoulders. She grabbed my hand and squeezed it. Her brown eyes were wet but not sad. It was so good to see her.

George and the physicians decided that we should visit the hospital before going to the hotel to see if our equipment had arrived. There we learned that our equipment had not cleared customs and was sitting in a Lima warehouse. Although the hospital agreed to make efforts to have the equipment delivered to Arequipa as soon as possible, that could take days. The hospital did, however, offer to let us use their anesthesia equipment. Xavier, Dick, and Richard, another anesthesiologist, examined the hospital's equipment and, after thorough testing and a comprehensive review of the equipment's sterilization records, agreed the hospital's equipment was safe and adequate.

If the hospital's anesthesia equipment had been unacceptable, our mission would have been scrubbed. The problem could have been prevented if George, as mission coordinator, had made arrangements to arrive in Peru a few days in advance to ensure that our equipment, which was necessary to do surgery, had cleared customs.

This is always a concern of medical missions around the world, that equipment sent ahead arrives in time. If a mission is aborted, the costs are phenomenal, not to mention that organizations need to explain a funded-then-aborted mission to donors and contributors. Also, CSI's policy was to not give in-country hospitals any financial assistance for use of their facilities. Had the hospital received some funds for allowing us to use the facility, the administrator, Esmeralda, may have been eager to get our equipment released and shipped. As it was, our own equipment arrived for the last two days of the mission.

# CHAPTER 14

# Libreria Diana

On Friday afternoon, when our bus finally arrived at the Casa Andina Hotel, many familiar faces welcomed us, and the hotel hosted our lunch. Tom and I were pleased to know that the rest of the afternoon was time on our own before we left for Juliaca in the morning. We looked forward to catching up with Liz.

We settled into our hotel room, and Liz came with us. As we unpacked, Liz sat on our bed and talked a mile a minute, jumping from topic to topic. I knew how she felt. We hadn't seen each other in a year, and although we emailed and talked often, we both had much to share. Because we had learned that Liz was the only student of eighty-five in her class who did not have a computer, we brought along a laptop that Tom planned to use on the mission and then leave with her. Liz was thrilled with it.

She was excited to tell us about her classes. "I love biostatistics, and I got 15 on a neurology exam," she said. "Final exams are in two weeks, and I'm not worried." She smiled, laughed, and talked with confidence and assurance that I had not seen before.

"You are really into the swing of medical school again. Are all of your classes on campus at the university?" I asked.

"Yes. And I want to take you there to show you where I have my classes. One of my professors is working in his office today, and I would like you to meet him. Can we do that this afternoon, Mamita?"

"Yes, yes, Liz, of course," I said.

"And on the way, I would like to go to the Libreria Diana. This is

76

where I buy some school supplies and where you have mailed things to me. My friend Elena and her husband Adel own it. They named the *libreria* after their daughter Diana. It is only a block from the university," Liz said.

As always, cabs were waiting in front of the hotel. Ronald stood by his taxi and smiled broadly.

"Hi, Ronald!" I yelled as I walked to him. "It's good to see you. You drove us last year, remember?"

He said he remembered, but I doubted it. After all, it had been a year, and how many American tourists must he have driven in his cab? Liz did her usual check. She looked in his cab to see his license displayed on the dashboard. Then she asked him in Spanish for the cost to take the three of us to the Liberia Diana near the Santa Maria University. He said the fare was eight soles, or $2.50.

"Okay, this is good," Liz said. "Tom, when you take cabs around Arequipa, please always look at the driver's license, which is right there." She pointed to the dashboard. "And always ask for the number of soles to the place you are going before you get in the cab."

"Got it," Tom said.

Liz sat in front, and Tom and I sat in the back. Tom chatted with Ronald, who responded in broken English. "We will be going to the hospital every morning," Tom told him. "Will you plan to take us each day?"

"Si, si, yes, I take you. I be here every morning to take you and your friends," Ronald said.

I was happy to see him again and shut my eyes for a moment to enjoy the good feelings from my past memories. I was also glad Ronald would be our driver and that we would all be in safe hands.

It was a fifteen-minute ride to the Libreria Diana. The bookstore was a small shop where students went to copy materials or buy pens and pencils. It did not, however, sell books. Rather, because textbooks are so expensive, students brought a shared text or photocopies to be photocopied for their own use. Liz also told us that receiving mail at her apartment was not reliable, so she used the Libreria Diana as her mailing address as did others.

Elena was from Mexico and Adel from Puno in Peru. They were in their midthirties and delightful. They spoke no English, so Liz interpreted in between my attempts to converse. They hugged us immediately and showed us their store. They were proud of it, and I could tell that Elena and Liz were close friends.

"Mamita," Liz said, "Elena has a gift that she and Adel have made for you."

Adel held out an alpaca tapestry he had made. It was about four feet by four feet and tightly woven in the typical Peruvian colors of red, black, orange, and green. It was beautiful.

"Elena says to tell you that Adel made this for you because you have been so kind to me," Liz said. "They have a farm here in Peru where they raise alpaca."

Tom and I were speechless. We wanted to pay them, but they refused and said they were so grateful for what we were giving to Liz. We visited for a while and, without speaking languages, our conversions were mostly friendly smiles, hugs, and nods to show our appreciation. I bought several birthday cards in Spanish that Elena wrote and sold at her store. It was another of many sweet and spontaneous moments in Peru.

Like many businesses in Peru, Libreria Diana was not succeeding, and Elena and Adel planned to return to Tijuana, Mexico, with their daughter. They believed they would have a better future with more possibilities for study and for business if they were closer to the United States.

We said goodbye and thanked them for their kindness. The tapestry Adel made hangs in our great room today. It reminds me of the many good people we met in Peru.

## CHAPTER 15

# Universidad Católica de Santa María

From the Libreria Diana, we walked to the university. Arequipa has many faces. The Plaza de Armas in the central city, not unexpectedly, is fronted by a centuries-old cathedral as well as dozens of other buildings reflecting the colonial city that it was. Elsewhere in the central city, with its generally narrow streets, are other striking colonial structures that have character but that are not always in good repair. The university campus had none of this architecture. The white stucco buildings were new and modern, three and four floors tall, and with large windows. In the building where Liz took several classes, the hallways were well lit and the floors marble. Classrooms were neat and orderly, and students and professors clustered in groups. It did not look anything like I expected, although I don't really know what I did expect. At the end of a hallway, we came to the office of one of Liz's professors. Liz knocked on the lovely mahogany and frosted glass door, and through it we saw the shadow of her professor as he rose from his desk.

As he opened the door, Liz greeted Dr. Noriega. He was a short man with thick, black hair and a rugged complexion. Wearing black-rimmed glasses and a white lab coat over a crisp blue dress shirt and a smartly colored red and white striped tie, he looked exactly like what I thought a medical professor should look like. Liz introduced us as close friends from the United States. He shook our hands, and we exchanged greetings in Spanish. He motioned for us to sit in chairs across from his desk. Dr.

Noriega spoke no English, but Liz translated. We told him we were impressed with the university, which seemed to please him. Tom asked what he taught, and he responded that he was the current head of the medical faculty and that he taught molecular biology and biochemistry. I said that I knew Liz was working hard and was committed to medical school. Liz blushed as she translated his response, particularly when he said that she was a good student and confirmed that she was working hard. We shook hands and said goodbye. Liz told us later that Dr. Noriega was very strict and often did not consider the students' opinions.

"He does not always approach us in a way that is helpful. He has a firm way of answering questions and does not want to discuss any other opinion on a topic. But what can I do, Mamita? It is medical school, so I deal with it."

I was glad to hear Liz say that. She was still at the beginning of her medical school journey, and I was glad she was realistic. Not all professors would be easy to work with.

From Dr. Noriega's office, we went to the administrative offices, where Liz dropped off some papers. We met Dr. Jacinta Torres, dean of the medical faculty and Liz's biology, cytology, and histology professor. We visited with Dr. Torres in our best broken Spanish while Liz put her papers in a tray on another desk. Some students saw Liz, and they greeted each other and began chatting and smiling.

It was Friday, and students were bustling everywhere. The campus was lined with colorful, blooming gardens and well-manicured shrubs. It was fall in Arequipa, and I was surprised there were so many flowers. Before we left campus, Tom and I used the restrooms, which were clean and bright. But I was quickly reminded that I was in Peru. There were no toilet seats.

That evening the three of us had an early dinner at the Aryquepay Restaurant on Jerusalem Street, where Liz and I had spent so many late evenings the year before and where I had heard the beginning of her story.

# CHAPTER 16

# Juliaca

The next day, Saturday, one team went to the hospital to evaluate Arequipa children whose parents had heard or read about our arrival. Another team of three doctors, Tom, an RN named Mary, a translator from Minneapolis named Claudia, Liz, and I took an early-morning Lan Peru flight to Juliaca in order to evaluate prospective patients from the remote city.

Juliaca, a city of perhaps two hundred thousand, is like no place I had imagined. At an altitude of nearly 12,500 feet, it is near Lake Titicaca, the highest freshwater lake in the world. Cattle raising, I'm told, is its predominant business. At that altitude, stepping from the airplane is quite literally breathtaking. The surrounding Andes Mountains are beautiful and inspiring, but the immediately obvious poverty distracts from nature's beauty. Driving through the community, we saw many small homes just partially built with three clay walls and a tarp for a roof. Yards were dirt peppered with sparse native plants and weeds. Barking dogs ran loose. Barefoot children in ragged clothing stood on the side of the dirt roads watching as our bus drove by while others played in mud puddles. There was no glass in most windows, and men and women sat on windowsills watching nothing. The unpaved streets were crowded with bicycles, pedicabs, and motored tricycle taxis. They zigged and zagged along the dirt streets, avoiding one another, the potholes, and random rocks that Tom said were the size of dogs. I never imagined such apparent poverty. If there was a place on earth that God forgot, I thought, it was Juliaca.

Our bus took us to a school where we used a large, vacant room to evaluate the children. The building was made of earth or thick concrete walls. While it was warming up outside, the dense walls kept the inside uncomfortably cold. There was no heat. We kept our sweaters and jackets on all the while, and still it was cold. Such buildings explained why, during the previous year's mission, mothers from Juliaca had kept their babies under layers and layers of blankets.

The indigenous people from this part of Peru are dark skinned, in part because of the sunlight at the high altitude. Most of the women dress in native attire and carry their babies on their backs until they learn to walk. For them, although there are some local physicians, access to health care is limited. Because the community is relatively isolated, there is a high rate of genetic intermarriage and, as a result, more birth defects than might otherwise be expected. Even so, the occurrence of cleft lip and palate defects is not exceptionally higher than in the United States, where such problems are almost always recognized and repaired in infancy.

We set up three stations. The first one obtained the children's and parents' names and took photographs for the medical record. Tom and Liz worked this station. At the second, Mary and I obtained each child's height, weight, vital signs, and medical history. At the third, doctors examined the child and determined which procedure was needed. One of the doctors spoke Spanish and Claudia translated as well, but they experienced some difficulty with the Quechua language. Liz, who spoke and understood Quechua, helped everywhere she could. The doctors decided whether the children, and the parents, would accompany us on the 150-mile bus ride that evening down and through the mountains to Arequipa for surgery.

Mrs. Huahuamello from the previous year's mission lived in Juliaca and came to the screening clinic with Nelida, who was now fifteen months old. She brought a friend who had a child with a cleft lip, hoping as Mrs. Huahuamello had hoped last year that her child would be selected for surgery. Liz and I talked to Mrs. Huahuamello, and she hugged me and began to cry. Liz did most of the talking. Nelida's father came this year and was holding Nelida. Her surgery had healed beautifully, and she ran around our makeshift clinic chattering, laughing, and playing with a dog-shaped plastic toy. It was bittersweet for me to see Nelida. I knew that because of her surgery, she would grow up with a normal appearance.

I also knew that Nelida's chance for a life outside poverty was unlikely. The thought made my eyes well up.

"I'm stepping outside for a minute," I said to Liz. I walked toward a cement bench opposite from where a long line of parents and children stood waiting to be screened in the hope that they would be selected. I sat down. The sun was bright, and the surrounding mountains were clear with bright shadows cast on them. I felt warm.

Liz followed me. "Are you okay, Mamita?" she said as she sat next to me and put her arm around my shoulders.

"Yes, Liz. Thank you. It makes me sad to think that last year we fixed little Nelida's cleft lip and now she's a beautiful child. But what hope does she have for any kind of a life here among all this poverty?"

"You are right, dear Liz. It is unlikely that Nelida will know any other way of life than how she lives here in Juliaca. But that is the way it is. She is better off because of her surgery. Her life will be better. That is enough."

Liz was right. And that is what I knew from other missions as well. The surgeries we provided made life easier and maybe gave the children and their families a future with some hope. Nelida looked like the other children and had a better chance for a normal life, to marry one day and have a family, or to do whatever was normal in this part of the world. I knew there were twenty-eight million people in Peru and more than half of them lived in poverty. My heart ached for Nelida.

Liz hugged me. We held hands as we walked back into the school building that was full of parents and children. Three teenage girls, age fifteen to eighteen, with severe cleft lips were next for screening. They were with their parents, but it appeared that they knew each other as well. If a cleft lip is not repaired early in childhood, the child grows into adolescence and the teenage years and the cleft becomes more exaggerated. When they approached Tom and Liz, one by one we saw that each wore a shawl and used it to cover her mouth. When it was time for Tom to take their picture, we saw how self-conscious, embarrassed, and shy they were.

Tom walked over to the first girl and gently touched her shoulder as she looked down at the ground. Liz translated.

"Do not be afraid or embarrassed," Tom said to the first girl. "The doctors need the picture, and we are here to help."

The girl looked at Tom and slowly drew the shawl away from her mouth. She made a thin smile as she looked kindly at Tom. She had a severe cleft lip. I said to Liz, "Those girls are so beautiful, and yet they feel like they have to cover their faces. That is so sad."

"They are very self-conscious because many people in the high country believe that they have a curse on them that made their face the way it is. We know that's not true, but these deformities make life very hard for teenage girls." Tom and I hoped the three girls would be selected. It would be the decision of the surgeons and a matter of how many cleft-lip patients could fit into our tight schedules.

We screened nearly one hundred children and teenagers that day. Meanwhile, the CSI team in Arequipa held about forty openings for Juliaca children. We crossed our fingers that the three teenage girls would be selected. The doctors had tough decisions to make, and they made them. By seven o'clock in the evening, they had selected those forty patients. A bus was chartered and within the hour the selected patients, their parents, and our CSI team boarded the coach for the 150-mile drive to Arequipa. Box dinners were provided and the coach was comfortable. Yet, despite our exhaustion, it was difficult to rest as the bus wended its way downward on what appeared to be a treacherous narrow road toward Arequipa. When we arrived, the patients and their families would stay in the homes of volunteers that CSI had arranged.

# CHAPTER 17

# Carlos

The next day, in Arequipa, was the second and final day for screening potential patients. Tom photographed children while Mary, Norrie from last year's mission, and I checked vital signs and quizzed parents about their children's overall health. Liz translated. The day went fast, and we finished by five thirty. Parents waited anxiously while the doctors finalized the schedule and then posted it on the hospital's front door. Unfortunately, some parents were crushed when their children's names weren't on the list.

Tom and I returned to the hotel. Liz arranged for us to have dinner with her and Carlos, who was now living in Arequipa. When we entered the restaurant, Carlos, a large man with black curly hair and gentle eyes, saw us at once, walked quickly toward us, hugged me tightly, and said in Spanish, "It is wonderful to finally meet you." Of course, we weren't hard to identify in Peru. Two very white Caucasians, with one being a blonde-haired woman, stand out in a Peruvian crowd. Tom and Carlos shook hands as Carlos pointed to our table, where Liz was standing. I hugged her. She looked beautiful in a brown leather jacket over a black sweater with tight, fitted jeans and black leather shoes. Her coal-black hair fell to her shoulders. She wore a little makeup, and her eyes sparkled. We ordered Pisco sours followed by saltado, the traditional favorite that Liz and I had enjoyed the year before that is prepared with chicken, peppers, onions, and seasoning; served on rice; and topped with a few french fries. This was Tom's first taste of Peruvian saltado.

Tom was interested to learn about Carlos's work, and Liz translated.

"I had a construction company. Among several building structures, my company built the railway station at Machu Picchu," Carlos said. "But as time went on, the corruption and bribes were more than I could handle or afford. It became difficult to get construction contracts without paying off bribes, and I had to give up."

"That's too bad," Tom said. "And yet I know this happens in many places and in the US as well. What did you do afterward?"

"In recent years I've worked in banking in Arequipa and Lima, helping people with paperwork in order to secure a loan," Carlos said. "This has been difficult because sometimes the bank pays employees for work they complete and other times not. This is the reason it has been hard for me to help Liz with medical school." He looked at her, reached over, and touched her hand.

Carlos's life had not been easy. He'd had many health issues, including a heart attack that contributed to his leaving the construction business. We learned that he had completed work for a number of companies where when payday came workers weren't paid or were told their pay was coming the next week, which may or may not have happened. He said that this was not uncommon in Peru.

While we waited for our food, Carlos continued. "It is amazing what you are doing for Liz. Her attending medical school is wonderful because in this way she will be helping the people here. And as you know, she has had a dream since she was a young girl to become a doctor." He had a warm smile and was easy to like.

He was also a miracle in Liz's life. Sometimes she referred to him as her godfather, other times as her uncle. He had two children from a marriage that had ended in divorce. This amazing man must have seen the pain and hurt in Liz's heart as she grew up. He believed in her, saw her commitment and capabilities, and helped her as best he could.

"What kind of work would you like to do? What would it be?" Tom asked.

"I would like to own a restaurant, a place where I could offer good and easy Peruvian food," he replied with enthusiasm. "A place where people can come to congregate and visit. Something like this restaurant but maybe less sophisticated."

"That's interesting," Tom said as he leaned back in his chair. "Have you managed a restaurant before?"

"No, but I have managed businesses. And I have managed workers in construction and at the banks."

The evening was enjoyable. We said good night but not goodbye because we knew we would see him again. Back at our hotel, Tom said, "I wish there were some way we could help Carlos. Not sure what that is, but it just seems like helping him could also help Liz."

"I agree. Liz told me in his recent jobs he's not made much money. But he might be a smart businessman if given the opportunity."

"Well, nobody makes much money in Peru unless they're born into wealth," Tom said. "There are strong social class distinctions. A few are very wealthy. Some others have decent jobs and live comfortable lives, but the majority are poor, and as we saw in Juliaca, many are extremely poor."

For Carlos, health issues made matters worse since he had no health insurance to receive the care or medications he needed. As was the case with many Peruvians, there was not much hope for change. At least Liz was studying to be a doctor. She would have professional status and earn more than if she had no career. That thought comforted me as I tried to sleep. Well, it somewhat comforted me. *Maybe there's something else*, I thought.

## CHAPTER 18

# Carlos Quispe? Where Is Carlos Quispe?

The following day, Monday, was the first day of surgeries. Sami Tholen, a surgical nurse and the wife of plastic surgeon Dick Tholen, also on this mission, and I co-coordinated nursing and patient care. My responsibilities were to ensure that the patients were ready and were brought to Sami's surgery unit on time. With fourteen cases scheduled daily, organization was essential.

Liz usually met us in the morning at the hospital and left around noon to attend her classes. On this first day, Liz and Tom identified patients from our surgical list and put wristbands on them. A nurse practitioner on our mission named Maria Rubin worked with Norrie and me on the pre- and postop nursing unit. Maria was Peruvian, born in Lima, but her family had moved to the United States when she was young. Later, she became a nurse and then a nurse practitioner. She worked at a Hispanic clinic in Minneapolis. Maria participated in many medical missions, and she, Tom, and I connected right away. She understood Peruvians and believed that they needed to help themselves because no one in Peru would do it for them. At the same time, she was most caring and compassionate. She also understood that when we asked Peruvians a question, we did not always receive a truthful answer. Instead, they told us what they thought we wanted to hear.

We assigned children to the wards with three, six, or eight beds and with each child's full name taped to the bed so Tom could easily identify them. That wasn't always possible because children ran about the room or moved from bed to bed. When Tom entered a room with his list of scheduled patients, he called out the name of the next child scheduled to have surgery. It sounded simple.

"Carlos Quispe, Carlos Quispe, please. Where is Carlos Quispe?" Tom called out loudly to be sure he was heard above the chattering children and parent conversations. Frequently, all of the parents raised their hands. Throughout the day, Tom called out Carlita Perez or Jose Rodriquez or Maria Lopez, and all the parents raised a hand and said, "Aquí! Aquí estamos! (Here! Here we are!)"

It was funny and a little frustrating, but Liz and Maria understood it all too well.

"You see," Liz said to Tom, "these parents know there is a schedule of surgeries for each day and that sometimes the cases take longer and the schedule gets behind. They are afraid they will be told there's no time for their child and they will be sent home."

"But if the schedule is behind, then we'd simply move that child to early the next morning," Tom said.

"Yes, *we* know that," she added, "but the parents are afraid. They have come this far and would be brokenhearted if the day is coming to a close and their child's name has not been called."

It made sense, and it helped us be patient when parents, especially as the afternoon wore on, asked, "Is it time for my child yet? Will I hear you say my child's name soon?" It helped us understand, but it made me sad too. Tom was wonderful and recalled enough Spanish to be consoling and comforting to the parents as he went in and out of patients' rooms, always checking wristbands and offering smiles of support as parents waited, holding on tightly to their babies and their hope.

The following afternoon, Liz came to the hospital after classes to help until we finished. Norrie said we were running out of infant diapers. Without a second thought, Tom and Liz left the hospital, hailed a taxi, and told the driver to take them to a local store. They purchased diapers while Maria, Norrie, and I continued to check patients' postop vital signs and administered antibiotics and pain medications. Then, at 2:32 p.m., the hospital walls shook and the furniture and beds rattled and slid around the room. Mothers screamed and children cried. We were in an earthquake—a big one.

The patients' and mothers' safety was our first concern. Mothers, children, and patients wept and wailed. Maria took over. She spoke in Spanish and in a calm yet authoritative voice that commanded the attention of all. "Mothers, get your children and move under a doorway," she said loudly. "Do it now! Everything is fine. It will be over soon! Move now and move quickly. Here are bottles of water for your babies. That's right. Move quickly!"

Maria moved throughout the rooms of mothers and children, patting them on the back and on their babies' behinds, repeating, "Everything will be fine. Be still now. It will be over soon."

Maria helped all of us. She was a rock, and she was right.

I remember thinking, *Am I going to die?* I felt sick and lonely at the thought, and at the same time, I closed my eyes and hoped that Tom and Liz were safe.

The shaking ended, although not as soon as I had hoped. Beds, cribs, and desks had slid in many directions, but the hospital stood. We later learned that the quake was a 7.8 on the Richter scale and that the epicenter was in the Región de Tarapacá in northern Chile, just three hundred miles south of Arequipa. Widespread damage had occurred throughout the mountain villages and killed several people. In Arequipa, there was damage to a few buildings. The hospital damage included cracks in the walls and some collapsed plaster. Over the following days, everyone talked about the earthquake, and we were relieved that the results were not more serious. Tom and Liz returned. During the quake, they were in a taxi at an intersection with hanging stoplights. The lights swayed heavily, and all traffic stopped. Tom said he and Liz were not afraid. I also knew from my years living in California and experiencing periodic earthquakes that the feeling is not as dramatic when you're outdoors. Being in a building during an earthquake, you feel more motion. Tom and I talked about the earthquake later and tried to imagine the devastation to a city the size of Arequipa if the epicenter had been closer. I put the thought out of my mind. Our mission was just beginning.

# CHAPTER 19

# Tres Hermosas Chicas

The next day, as usual, we arrived at the hospital early and were thrilled to see that the three teenage girls from Juliaca were on the day's schedule for cleft-lip repairs. We remembered that they had come to the screening together, so when we admitted them to the hospital, I made sure that they shared a room with three beds so they could have the security of being together. The doctors performed their surgeries that afternoon and consecutively. The next morning, they were alert and ready for discharge to their parents and the local volunteers who had lovingly opened their homes to host them.

We agreed that we would give each of the three girls a mirror so they could see for the first time how they looked following the life-changing surgery. Late in the morning, Liz arrived for a couple of hours between her classes, and she, Tom, and I knocked on the door of their room.

"Buenas dias," Tom said cheerfully. "Aquí hay tres hermosas chicas!" (Here are three beautiful girls!)" The girls did not cover their faces but smiled and giggled, their surgical incisions in full view. With Liz translating, each of us sat on the side of one of their beds. "We have a mirror for you to see how beautiful you look," Liz said. "It is your choice, but we think you will be very happy with what you see." Now Liz giggled. Her comforting voice relaxed all of us.

The three girls looked at and nodded to one another, and then they looked at Tom, Liz, and me and nodded. "Si, si," they said. Then they agreed they would all look in their mirrors at the same time. We handed each of them a mirror. They looked at their faces, and each girl dropped her jaw just slightly as she saw her new face. They smiled and squealed with delight as they glanced to one another and then back at themselves in the mirror. With tears in their eyes, they looked at us—for approval, perhaps—and we saw the joy, maybe relief, on their faces. There were tears and smiles all around. It was a powerful moment. We saw faces changed for life.

# CHAPTER 20

# Sofia

I recalled a phone conversation from before we came to Peru the second time, when Liz had told me tearfully, "My mother called to ask me to come to see her. I did it because, even though it has been many years since we talked, she is my mother, and I so very much want the pain in my heart to go away. I hoped maybe this time it would be different."

I told Liz, "You did the right thing. People can change. It has been many years. She has had a lot of time to think about how the decisions she made where you were concerned have affected you."

But it wasn't different. Liz tried to have a nice conversation with Sofia, but it turned ugly, as Liz said it always did. Sofia called her a "rebel girl" for not visiting, for not obeying her mother, and for not continuing to work as a hairdresser. The visit was short, and Liz left, again promising herself that she would not go back.

Now, on Wednesday afternoon at the hospital, Liz told Tom and me that her mother, who knew Liz was in medical school, wanted to meet us. *How ironic,* I thought. Sofia gave Liz to her mother to raise, took her back, ignored her, gave her away again, told her she was too stupid to go to medical school and that the only thing she could do was be a hairdresser. Now good things were happening for Liz, and suddenly Sofia wanted to meet the people who were making it all possible.

Part of me wanted to meet Sofia, the mother of the person who I was now beginning to see as my own daughter. Another part of me wanted to not intrude in the relationship, such as it was. But I wanted it to be the best for Liz.

"Do you want us to meet her, Liz?" I asked.

"Yes, I think I do. She and my sister Lydia will be here this afternoon," Liz said in a sad voice. I knew that seeing Sofia was painful and reminded her of the past.

"Well, then, let's meet for a short visit." Still, I had mixed feelings about this woman who had hurt Liz and scarred her for life.

It was midafternoon, and all the patients had gone to surgery. We had a lull before the children would return from recovery. Sofia, Lydia, Liz, Tom, and I went into an empty patient room. Liz translated.

Sofia was a short, dark-skinned woman with deep-set brown eyes and black hair. I didn't see any of Liz's features in her. Lydia looked more like Sofia. I suspected that Mateo, Liz's father, was more of native descent and Sofia more Spanish. Sofia's smile seemed forced, and she made no eye contact. *Do you know that your daughter told me about your maternal shortcomings?* I thought.

Sofia came to me sobbing and saying in Spanish that she appreciated all that I was doing for Liz. She said that Liz was a wonderful daughter and put her arm around her. Liz looked at the floor. I tried my best to tell Sofia in Spanish that Tom and I think Liz is wonderful too. I said that we love Liz and that she is an amazing young woman. I must have done a good job because Liz blushed. Then I thanked Sofia for coming to meet us. Tom took a few pictures of Sofia, Liz, Lydia, and me. When I looked at the pictures, Liz was not smiling. She told me later that Sofia's emotions were not genuine and that she thinks if she sobs and cries, Tom and I will be impressed with her. Liz was unsettled by the meeting.

At one point when Liz was translating, Sofia looked at me hard, and I wondered if for a moment she realized that she really did have an amazing daughter. After pleasantries, Liz told us that Lydia made us a drawing of the Misti volcano so we would remember Arequipa. Lydia handed it to me as if it were a precious jewel. She was delightful. Then she hugged me tightly and said in Spanish, "Thank you for everything you are doing for my sister. You and your husband are angels to our world."

I thanked her for her drawing, and she signed her name at the lower right corner of the picture. Liz spoke briefly with her mother and sister and then turned to us. "They are leaving now," she said. "My mother wants to say thank you again for all you have done for me."

Then Sofia hugged me again. I saw tears in her eyes, and she repeated many times, "Gracias. Gracias para todo. (Thank you. Thank you for everything.)"

Sofia and Lydia left the patient unit, and I was glad to see them go. I felt it was an artificial exchange. I put my arm around Liz and gave her a squeeze. We returned to our patients and began checking vital signs and talking with the mothers. Liz chattered baby talk in Spanish with a fussy child, and I wrote on a patient's chart at the desk on the other side of the room. I looked up and saw Liz walk to the window near a child's crib. She picked up the child, sat, and rocked the child. I saw she had tears in her eyes. She started to get up when our eyes met. Liz looked at me and smiled as she wiped her tears. She smiled, nodded, and mouthed, "I am fine, Mamita." Then, she placed her hand over her heart, a gesture I had seen her do often when she expressed gratitude. She was moving forward with her life, and I intended to be there for her.

# PART 4

## Change of Plans and Disappointment

# CHAPTER 21

# A Room With No View

Days at the hospital were long while Norrie, Maria, and I worked later into the evenings to ensure that the patients were stable before turning them over to the Peruvian nurses on the night shift. Mary, the RN who accompanied us to Juliaca was working mostly in the recovery area. Although procedures were generally uneventful, one young boy went into respiratory distress following surgery. This required that he be placed in intensive care with round-the-clock attention. The pediatricians and all the nurses pitched in, and each of us, including Norrie, Maria, and I, covered the child's care for many hours over two days and nights until he was stable. It was grueling hours for all of us on top of our regular hours in surgery or postop, but well worth it when the child returned to the pediatric unit.

For relief, we agreed that each of us would have one evening when we left early to catch up on sleep or socialize with our colleagues. I was scheduled to leave early on Thursday, when we planned to have Liz show us her apartment and then go to dinner with Carlos and her.

Back at the hotel, Tom and I changed out of scrubs and cleaned up. Liz arrived by taxi at five. The three of us then took a cab to her apartment on Calle Samuel Velarde. From the outside, the three-story red-brick building had charm. Through the entrance was an open staircase to all three floors. Carlos and his elderly mother, Yola, owned two apartments in the building. One was on the first floor, where Yola lived, and the other, on the second, was where Liz lived rent free.

As Liz opened her door, she smiled, and I could tell she was proud to be showing us her apartment. It had three rooms separated not by doors but by arches. To the left was a small area that Liz used as a kitchen. It had a sink, a countertop, and a small hotplate. There was no refrigerator. To the right was a small room with a wooden chair, but otherwise it was empty. A dim yellow light bulb hung from a cord in the center and swung when Liz pulled the string to turn it on. Farther right through an archway was a double bed, a small dresser, and a table holding a small reading lamp and several books. A bookshelf filled with books of all sizes was against the wall, and more lay on the bed. Three poles held Liz's clothes. The paint was medium gray in the bedroom and tan elsewhere. The overall appearance was dreary, partly due to poor lighting. Newspaper covered the only small window.

"Why the newspaper?" I asked.

"It is because the apartments that are on the other side of the building can see into my apartment. I have no view from that window, so I use newspapers to cover it." Liz replied sadly. I pulled out an edge of the newspaper. She was right. From that window, I could see into other apartments in the building, and obviously people in those apartments could see into hers. It made the room dark and bleak, I thought, but I didn't say so.

"I think your place is cozy and comfortable," I said, probably unconvincingly. "And it's wonderful that Carlos lets you live here without paying rent. He has given you so much."

"Yes, it works for me now," she replied. "My uncle—he is like you and Tom, who are special gifts in my life." She looked down and clasped her hands together, almost as if praying.

"But," I said, looking around the apartment again, "where is your *baño*? I don't see a shower or toilet."

She turned away. "Dear Liz, I do not have a baño. There is one downstairs that the tenants have to share."

Forgetting that in the United States it had not been so many years since many people lived in rooming houses with shared baths, I said, "No baño? But what if you have to use the bathroom at night? Do you have to go downstairs to the toilet?"

She began to cry. I went to her and hugged her tightly. In that moment,

I thought of the young Liz, the girl who cried by herself after being left alone with no one to console her.

"Liz, I'm sorry," I said as she cried in my arms. "It never occurred to me that you didn't have a baño. I'm afraid I put my foot in my mouth."

She looked up at me, and behind her tears, she smiled.

"Si, Mamita, I know what you are saying." She wiped her eyes and then continued. "It is a funny English expression about the foot in the mouth. I have heard it before."

"I wasn't thinking when I said that," I said.

"Come sit here next to me, Mamita," she said.

I obeyed. We sat on her bed, and she reached both her small hands out to hold mine.

"Dear Mamita, you do not do this. You do not put the foot in your mouth." She giggled softly. "You are learning that we are from different worlds. My world is of poverty with much less, but I have never known anything else either. However, we Peruvians still have a lot to give to this world."

"That's true," I said. "And you are helping me understand your world."

As we stood, I walked over to the window with no view and stared at the newspaper. I felt numb as I realized that the poor girl with the sad eyes had taught me something. Since I had met Liz the previous year, I had been curious about her apartment but had never imagined that she didn't have a toilet. But then I hadn't asked either.

When I turned around, Tom was standing in the area where Liz had a hot plate and a sink.

"I see that you don't have a refrigerator," he said quietly. "Do you share with another apartment?"

"No, I just buy what I need for a day or two."

"That's okay," Tom said, "but not very efficient. Do you know of an appliance store where we can go tomorrow? I'd like to buy you a small refrigerator. Can I do that for you, Liz?"

"Si, dear Tom." Liz put her arm around his waist. "That will be very kind of you." She paused and then added, "You know, it is not much what I have here, but it okay. I am content."

*Yes*, I thought, *that's another thing*. She said that often. She had nothing, and she was content with what I considered to be barely getting by with the necessities of life. Few people I knew were content with what they had. Everyone, including myself, was always looking for and expecting more—more money, more material things, more to do with our time. As she said this to us, I looked at her and felt some envy. *How could this young woman be so content,* I thought, *and have so little?* As she spoke these words so convincingly, I smiled as I saw the little girl with the sad eyes become a young woman whom I now loved as if she were my own daughter.

The following day I worked at the hospital all day. Liz had morning classes but met Tom in the afternoon. They walked a few blocks down Jerusalem Street to the Plaza de Armas, where there was an appliance store, a small version of a Best Buy. The saleswoman was very helpful but spoke no English. Liz translated and described what they were looking for. She chose a small refrigerator, the size that many college students in the United States have in their dorm rooms. The salesperson happily set up a free delivery for the following day in the late afternoon so Liz could be home when it arrived.

Back at the hotel, Tom said, "I keep thinking how many people were in the appliance store today. There were young people Liz's age shopping seriously and carefully for televisions and appliances. There *are* people in Peru who can afford to buy some things. Unfortunately, there are too many people like Liz Cardona who can't afford to buy anything."

# CHAPTER 22

# Team Dinner

As they had the year before, the hospital hosted the closing event to celebrate the conclusion of our mission. The Peruvian doctors and nurses and the entire American team gathered this time in a large conference room. Tom, Liz, and I sat in the second row among many of the nurses and engaged in conversation, in both Spanish and English, with Liz once again translating.

We enjoyed Inca Kola, Liz's favorite local beverage and one that Tom had a taste for as well. To me, it's excessively sweet. "This Inca Kola is like nothing we have at home," Tom said. "Liz, I think I'm going to have you send me a case." Liz and Tom laughed, and their interaction warmed my heart. Tom embraced the entire journey I was on with Liz, and he supported us both from the first day I had told him her story. At that moment, watching him with Liz, I loved him more than ever.

Thank-yous were exchanged. Liz was embraced by both the Peruvian and American teams, and Esmeralda thanked Liz for translating for the Americans. *Miracles do happen,* I thought as I watched Esmeralda speak kindly to Liz. We all received certificates of appreciation and commemorative lapel pins.

"I am so happy to be here and be part of this wonderful afternoon," Liz said to me with a huge smile on her face.

"You deserve it. You've been a huge help to all of us." We sat next to each other, and I put my arm around her. She glanced down at the document she had received. It read, "To express our appreciation and our gratitude for service to the patients at the Honorario Delgado Hospital."

I noticed that she had already attached the lapel pin to her lab coat. I thought that she probably had never received this kind of recognition and appreciation from so many people.

"But dear Liz," she said, "you have really made all this possible just as you are making my medical school a reality. I wish I could become a doctor in the States. Then I could be with you all of the time. Perhaps I can find a way to apply to a medical school in the US."

"Well, that's an interesting thought," I answered. "I don't know much about the current application process for international students to apply to a US medical school, but I suppose we can look into that."

George arranged the final team dinner for six o'clock at a restaurant near the Plaza de Armas in central Arequipa. This time Liz was included. She arrived at our hotel at five thirty. It was a cool but beautiful evening, so everyone decided to walk the eight blocks together from our hotel to the restaurant. Waiters escorted us upstairs to a large private dining room. The place settings were lovely with red china, water glasses and wineglasses, flatware, and colorful table napkins. Pisco sours were served. We agreed that it was good to see one another in attire other than our scrubs and surgical caps. The restaurant served us platters of aji-chili-spiced shrimp, crab, and a whitefish in a tomato-based sauce, spicy pork tenderloin, sliced alpaca with potatoes, steamed vegetables, plates of corn bread, and, for dessert, a bread pudding Chincha-style. We enjoyed Peruvian red wine throughout the dinner. Everyone intermingled, and conversation blended in Spanish and English.

Liz was enjoying herself. We sat next to each other with Tom across from Liz. All the doctors and nurses, including Esmeralda, came to her, pulled up chairs, and asked her about medical school. She beamed as she described her classes.

I thought about how far Liz and I had come on our journey and particularly how much Liz's life had changed in just a year. But Liz had changed my life too. I saw my priorities differently. I was beginning to understand how poverty affects people, and I was sad to be leaving Liz and Peru the next day. But I felt joy, too, at the thought of Liz's commitment to become a doctor and our commitment to her. Although she still had three and a half years of medical school followed by an internship, seeing her enjoy herself made it all seem real.

By eleven o'clock, people started leaving. The Peruvian doctors and nurses had to work the next day, and our team would leave for home. A small group of us planned to fly to Cusco to spend three days there and at Machu Picchu before returning to Minnesota. As we waited at the curbside for cabs, I asked Liz if she had been to Cusco and Machu Picchu.

"No, Mamita, I have not been there," she replied, but this time she did not lower her head as if she were ashamed. "I have not been to any places in Peru except Lima and also Tacna, which is near Aplao where I lived as a little girl. I have been to Juliaca now, and when I was working earlier, I was in Chile."

When a cab stopped, she checked to see the license of the driver and ask the number of soles to ride to the Casa Andina hotel. With acceptable answers, Tom, Liz, Dick, Sami, and I squeezed in one cab.

"Where's George?" I asked.

"He's paying the bill," Dick said. "He said it was taking a while and for us to go ahead."

Back at the hotel, we gathered in the empty dining room. Some of the doctors had beer and others of us wine as we reminisced about our mission and talked about going home. Liz joined the conversation, and we sat and talked until after one in the morning.

"Did anyone see George come back?" Sami asked. Someone suggested that he probably had gone straight to his room, and no one gave much thought to not seeing him. He was independent and frequently off on his own. Liz said good night and hailed a cab back to her apartment.

She was adamant about coming back in the morning. "Tomorrow is the Father's Day in your country," she said. "It is important that I see you and Tom also before you go back to the US. I will be here at ten o'clock."

# CHAPTER 23

# Kidnapped

Our flights to Cusco and to Lima conveniently left at two o'clock in the afternoon. Most of us met in the dining room at seven in the morning. We ate breakfast, and Tom had a final taste of cold-cut alpaca.

When Dick Tholen came into the dining room, he looked worried. "George didn't come back to the hotel last night," he said. "Xavier and I talked with the front desk, and they checked his room. He didn't sleep in his bed. The restaurant where we ate last night is closed, so we can't ask if anyone saw him leave there."

Minutes later, thinking George may have gone to the hospital to make sure equipment was packed and ready to ship home, Dick and Xavier left to talk with Esmeralda. They returned to the hotel around nine thirty after learning nothing. At about the same time, George arrived with a harrowing story.

After paying the restaurant, George decided to walk back to the hotel. He was a man of about sixty-five years, trim and fit, gray-haired, and distinguished looking. Three blocks into the eight-block walk back to the hotel, a car drove alongside him.

"Need a taxi, mister?" the driver said in broken English.

It was late and dark. George was tired. Riding back to the hotel now sounded like a good idea, so he got in the back seat of the car. The car drove two blocks and turned sharply into a narrow alley. Before he knew what was happening, two men opened the back doors, one on each side, and jumped in next to George. They spoke no English, and George neither spoke nor understood a word of Spanish. They drove to an ATM, and the two men in the back seat pulled him out of the car and yelled, "PIN! PIN!" They knocked George around and continued to hit and push him as they yelled commands.

George didn't know what they were saying, but he knew what they wanted. He attempted to enter his PIN at the ATM, but the machine didn't work. Many of us had learned this was common in Peru. One ATM worked; another didn't. We had no idea why.

Now the kidnappers, believing George had entered a false PIN, became angry but could not communicate with their hostage. They forced him to give them his gold wedding ring and an expensive watch. They drove to another ATM. This time George's PIN worked, and he withdrew $200, his per-day limit. The kidnappers then forced him to the floor of the back seat and drove around Arequipa while hitting and kicking him. At five in the morning, the captors stopped and pushed him out of the car, roughed up and shaken but grateful to be alive. Dawn was approaching. He had no idea where he was, but since he saw farms, a coffee plantation, and fields, he knew he was in the country. He walked toward what he thought would be a populated area and began to see buildings. He hailed a taxi and told the driver to take him to the Arequipa Police Station. Following considerable questioning and paperwork, the police drove George to the Casa Andina.

When he told his story, we were amazed that he wasn't more shaken. The incident pointed out that all of Liz's concerns about checking out the license of the cabbies was well founded. George, of course, had made two mistakes. He had been out alone late at night, and he hadn't verified the taxi's legitimacy. It was just about money, of course. But this robbery could have turned more violent and even fatal. I thought how devastating this incident could have been, not only for George and his family but also for the many nonprofit organizations that travel the globe providing medical services.

The kidnapping was in the newspaper the day after the incident as well as highlighted on the local television station. The headline read: *Medical Missionary Kidnapped near Restaurant in Central City.* The article described our group and why we were in Arequipa. The community was outraged, and concern for our mission and for CSI was great. George was lucky indeed. He said he was looking forward to going home, and none of us blamed him.

# CHAPTER 24

# Leaving Arequipa

Later that morning, as promised, Liz came to the hotel for a final goodbye. Carlos was with her. The four of us went to a nearby restaurant for a light lunch before our bus headed to the airport.

Tom and Liz waited for their Inca Kola, and Carlos and I ordered bottled water. "Dear Tom," Liz said as she reached over and touched his hand. "You have been like a father to me during this time together. You have supported me and have shown me your love. For that I want you to know that I love you, and I want you to have a happy Father's Day."

Tom had tears in his eyes as Liz presented him with a Father's Day card—in Spanish, of course. The sentiment was loving and sweet.

He put his arm around her. "I'm happy we can help you, and we've had a great time these past ten days. You're doing a good job in school, and we're proud of you." We had brought the laptop computer with us and gave it, as well as an envelope with $300, to her. "Here's your computer," I said. "We changed the language to Spanish, so it should be good to go for you. And here's some extra money." We hugged, and Liz held back the tears.

"Thank you so very much, Mamita for all you are doing. *Te quiero mucho, Mamita.* (I love you very much, Mother.)"

"Yo también te quiero mucho" I replied, and we hugged for what seemed like a long time.

That afternoon, Tom and I flew to Cusco to tour the city and then rode the tourist train to visit Machu Picchu for a day. On the plane returning to Minnesota, we reminisced about our days at the hospital, the *tres hermosas chicas*, and George. But mostly we talked about time with Liz and Carlos, her apartment, her translating for us, and her amazing determination.

# CHAPTER 25

# Change of Plans

After returning from Peru, Tom and I spent hours reliving our experiences with the children and our days and evenings with Liz. I was relieved that she was doing well and thrilled to see how her life had changed from the year before. I knew that my paying for her medical school made the change possible, but Liz was doing the heavy lifting. When I saw her smiling, laughing, and being self-confident, I felt good. Her hopeless and helpless condition would soon all be in the past.

At the same time, I felt unsettled. Liz had four-and-a-half years left of medical school plus an internship. Still, her grades, while passing, weren't outstanding. And she would be thirty-seven when she finished her internship. I still wasn't sure about the requirements for a residency program in Peru. If Liz needed to complete the SERUMS and a residency, that would add another couple of years. Only then could she earn a professional salary—good by Peruvian standards but no king's ransom. Although I could shut my eyes and hear Liz say, "It is not much what I have here, but I am content," I was beginning to feel that as much as I wanted her to finish medical school, I wanted her out of poverty as well.

"Liz seems to be doing pretty well at school," Tom said. "Her life is changed, and she'll be a fine doctor. She's a good listener, and she's compassionate and caring."

"But I'd like to see her complete school in less time," I said. Then, expressing a thought that I had been having, I added, "If she were in the US, she could have more doors open to her. Do you think she could apply for medical school at the University of Minnesota?"

109

"Probably not," Tom said. "A medical school in the United States would require our equivalent to a bachelor's degree before applying. And medical school would cost far more in the US than what you're wiring her now. I know there are student visas," Tom added. "And it's most likely true that she'd earn a better income if she studied here and then worked here. She could probably stay if she did something that's in short supply— maybe nursing. Then, if she wanted to, she might later become a nurse practitioner like Maria or a nurse anesthetist, but her earning power and living standard would be far greater than as a Peruvian doctor."

"That's true," I said. "And she wouldn't live in poverty. I don't think she knows what that would be like." I closed my eyes and tried to imagine what it would be like to have her living in the United States, probably with us.

"Let's look into what it takes to get a student visa," Tom said. "If Liz came over her summer break in December, she'd have time to decide if she wanted to stay or return to Peru."

"That's a great idea." I put my arm around Tom's shoulders.

We spent the next week checking websites for requirements and procedures to obtain a student visa. I talked to an immigration attorney, and we learned that, first, Liz would need to apply to a college or university and meet the requirements for admission. Then, if she were admitted, she could apply for a student visa.

Normandale College was close to where we lived, its admission procedure was straightforward, it had a two-year nursing program, and the cost was considerably less than the University of Minnesota. In addition, transportation to Normandale wouldn't pose a problem.

"In the meantime, she wouldn't be living in poverty," I added, unable to let go of that thought. "I'll approach the topic with her on our next phone conversation."

I went to sleep happy and could hardly wait to speak to Liz. I could hear the excitement in her voice when I brought it up the following evening.

"Oh, Mamita, that would be so amazing to be in the US and to study there and to be with you," she said. "I think it would be a special experience."

"It would take a lot of work on your part," I told her. "We learned that you will need to pass the TOEFL, the Test of English as a Foreign Language, but I am sure you can. Then you'll need to submit all of your college work from when you studied in Lima and from medical school in Arequipa. That will be evaluated by WES, the World Education Services. They'll decide what courses and grades from Peru will transfer here. You may already be close to a bachelor's degree.

"You'll need to complete paperwork on your end for admission to Normandale College, which is close to where we live. If you are accepted at Normandale, you can request the student visa."

Over the weeks that followed, we continued to talk and send emails on the subject of Liz's coming to the United States to study nursing. I explained the requirements. Then I asked, "Liz, what do you think? This is a big decision. Would you want a different career, or are you convinced that you want to study medicine in Peru?" I asked. "You need to think about this over the coming weeks."

"*Sí*, I know this is a big decision," Liz said. "I do have to think about it, but I know you are right about having a better life in the US. It is very hard here for people who are poor. Unless you are born into a family with money, nothing will ever change. I have known no other way. I don't like it, but I can't do anything about it."

"But maybe together we can help you do something about it, about getting out of poverty," I told her. "If you finished a nursing program, you could take another year to become a nurse practitioner. There are many options, and all of them would give you a very good income and all of them would be faster than staying in medical school."

"Yes, Mamita, I do understand. I know that I could have a better life. I could live with you for a while and then support myself. I have nothing to keep me in Peru, Mamita, nothing except my uncle. I talked with him, and he is very much in favor of me coming to the US."

"And Liz," I said, "you could come when you are finished with your classes this semester, in the middle of December. If you decide this is not what you want, you can go back to Peru and register for the next semester in medical school. You wouldn't lose any medical school time, and it would give you an opportunity to see what you think about the US."

Although I wanted Liz to really think about the idea, I wondered what she wouldn't like about living here. "You'd never be poor again," I said. "And you'd never be without your own baño."

Liz's conversations were convincing. Tom met with Antoinette Bowling-Harris, an admissions officer at Normandale Community College, who was particularly helpful and supportive. For weeks Tom worked to complete the paperwork and requirements on our end.

During telephone conversations and emails with Liz, we explained that she should draft a letter to go with her application to Normandale College and direct it to Mrs. Antoinette Bowling-Harris. During these conversations and emails, Liz referred to Mrs. Harris as Mrs. Antoinette. In her draft letter, she wrote, "Dear Mrs. Antoinette." I was used to this. She had addressed American women on our missions by "Ms." followed by their first names—Ms. Mary Alice, Ms. Peggy, and initially she called me Ms. Liz. During a telephone conversation with Liz, Tom tried to explain the correct way to address a woman in the United States.

"When you address a married woman in the United States," Tom said, "if you know her first name, you can use either Ms. or Mrs. and her last name. So she would be either Ms. Bowling-Harris or Mrs. Bowling-Harris. Sometimes married women still prefer to use their husband's first name. For example," Tom said, having no idea of his actual name, "if Mrs. Bowling-Harris's husband's name is James, she might be addressed as 'Mrs. James Bowling Harris.'" It was too much information.

"Okay, dear Tom, thank you for explaining this to me. I will change my letter to say, 'Dear Mrs. James Bowling Harris,'" Liz said with confidence.

Tom laughed. "But I don't *know* her husband's name. In your letter, just call her Mrs. Bowling-Harris. Do you understand that, Liz?"

"Yes, now I do." Liz laughed too, but Tom was reasonably sure she didn't know why.

We completed the paperwork for the college, and I sent Liz money to take the TOEFL exam, which she would do in Arequipa. The results would be sent directly to the college. Tom and I were surprised when Mrs. Harris called.

"We received the results of Elizabeth Cardona's TOEFL exam," she told Tom. "Ms. Cardona missed a passing score by one point. All of her paperwork is complete, but this is a hard decision. Technically she must pass the test in order to be granted a student visa and be accepted to the college."

Tom and Mrs. Harris had a long conversation about Liz's plans, her medical school courses, and her opportunities in the United States. Mrs. Harris understood Liz's situation and the circumstances of her poverty as well. She had heard similar stories from other out-of-country students and was a sympathetic supporter of international students. Within a few days, she called Tom again and agreed to accept Liz into the college. We were thrilled. I wired money for airfare, and on November 10, with college acceptance papers in hand, Liz went to Lima. She applied for and was granted a US student visa to come to the United States to begin classes at Normandale College in January 2006.

The weeks of research, paperwork, and meetings that Tom had completed, along with the buildup of anticipation and then the possibility of let down that Liz may not be accepted at Normandale, left us exhausted. At the same time, we were exhilarated when we learned that she would actually be coming. I thought of all the places I wanted to show her, the experiences I wanted to share with her—our local museums, the opera and symphony, the university. And of course, I wanted her to meet our family and friends.

The guest room on the lower level of our home would be her bedroom. In it was an antique cherry bedroom set that my parents had bought when they were married in 1937. It had delicate, dark-bronze hardware on the dresser and chest of drawers and a headboard with matching decorative patterns. I emptied the drawers, cut new shelf paper, and polished the wood. I packed away the books I had stored on the bookcase in the room that would be Liz's. As I did so, I imagined Liz's excitement at the thought of filling the shelves with her own books. I had a recent edition of *Taber's Cyclopedic Medical Dictionary*, a *Merck Manual,* and the new Mosby's *Nursing Drug Reference* that I placed on an upper shelf. I put a Peruvian doll I had bought on the way to Machu Picchu the previous spring on a shelf along with framed photos of Liz, me, Tom, and Carlos. There was plenty of space for the books she would need at Normandale. I wanted her to feel at home. Finally, I cleaned Liz's bathroom, just down the hall from her bedroom. I washed the floor and shower and put decorative artificial flowers in an antique vase that had been my mother's.

My mind wandered. I remembered how often my mother had said to me, "I'm sorry you didn't want to have children. You would have been a wonderful mother." I never agreed with her. I was always glad I had made the decision I did. But now I smiled as I thought of those words. I imagined my mother would be happy to know Liz Cardona was in my life.

On the same level was a large family room where we watched television, complete with a fireplace and kitchen area. I stocked the refrigerator with soft drinks and wine. In an adjacent room was a round table, chairs, and bookshelves. This area opened to a pond where we enjoyed ducks, geese, and other wildlife. I imagined Liz using this area for studying, watching television, and relaxing.

She was scheduled to fly on LAN Peru airlines from Arequipa to Lima and then take a Continental night flight from Lima to Houston and on to Minneapolis. I used my frequent flyer miles from business travel to buy the Continental tickets, and Liz bought her ticket on LAN Peru with money I sent. I booked a return flight for late February but felt confident she wouldn't use the ticket. I was certain she would be so happy in the United States that she would never want to go back to Peru and be poor again.

Liz and I talked daily about what she should bring to Minnesota and what she could leave in Peru.

"It's cold in Minnesota," I said. "We have a lot of snow right now, and more is expected. Bring warm clothing if you have it. Don't waste space with summer clothing. We'll get what you need next spring."

"And I'll bring my photos from our mission," Liz said excitedly. "I can't leave them in Peru."

"Yes, of course, and bring the camera I gave you, and your medical books," I added.

"Si. I do not have much but I will bring everything," Liz said. "Oh, and I do not have a warm coat. I will buy one for the trip with the money you sent."

The week before she was scheduled to arrive, many of my friends and family brought boxes to our house filled with gently used clothing, including slacks, sweaters, and even shoes in Liz's size four. Some purchased new items for her as well. Sami Tholen, Dr. Dick Tholen's wife, who had co-coordinated patient care on the 2005 mission with me, asked me to go shopping with her to buy some new clothes for Liz. Sami was generous with her purchases, and we had a great time imagining Liz, less than five feet tall, looking proud and beautiful in her new black tailored slacks and red sweater that Sami and I agreed would look wonderful with Liz's coal black hair.

In the days before Liz's arrival, I thought about how we had come into each other's lives. I knew that what I had been able to do had changed her life. What I was only now beginning to realize was the impact that Liz had on me. My priorities were changing. My focus was less on what I had and more on what I could give. I was learning and reading about the struggles that people of poverty face. I had a lump in my throat when I thought about that morning in Arequipa when a young woman with a perfect smile and tremendous gifts shook my hand and changed my world.

The morning of December 22, Liz and I talked one last time before she left Arequipa.

"Do you have everything packed, and are you ready for your journey?" I asked.

"Si, Mamita. I am ready, and everything is packed. I am so excited. My uncle Carlos is going with me to Lima and then will stay with me at the airport until I board the plane for Houston." She talked so fast I could hardly understand her.

"Tom and I will meet you at the Minneapolis airport tomorrow morning. I hope you can sleep on the flight to Houston," I said.

"I don't know if I will be able to sleep. I am so happy and excited." She laughed. Then she paused a long moment, and I thought I heard her crying softly.

"Are you okay, Liz?" I asked.

"Oh, yes, Mamita, I am very fine," she answered. "I am so happy; I do not know how to express it. When I think of coming to the US, to be with you, my Latin heart begins to sing like a bird!"

# CHAPTER 26

# Holidays

With airline tickets, student visa, and passport in hand, plus two checked suitcases, Liz boarded the Continental flight that brought her to Houston on December 23, 2005. She arrived at 6:20 a.m., had no problems at customs and immigration, and then walked through Houston's giant airport to the gate where she checked in for the flight to Minneapolis. She called me from the gate, just minutes before boarding.

"I'm here, Mamita, Isn't it wonderful?" She giggled.

"Yes, it is. Tom and I will meet you when you arrive in Minneapolis," I said. "Was everything fine when you left Lima? Was Carlos with you?"

"Yes, he was, and much to my surprise, so were my mother and my father and my sisters and my aunt Camilla," she said. "They wanted to see me off on the flight to the US."

"I'm sure you were surprised. You can tell me about it when you are here. We'll see you soon."

"That's interesting," I told Tom. "Liz's entire family saw her off."

"I'm not surprised," he said. "These are poor people whose daughter has a great opportunity, one they could only dream about. Of course, if she does well and stays in the US permanently, they hope Liz will send them money."

A few days earlier, I had called Continental Airlines at the Minneapolis-St. Paul airport and explained that I was going to be meeting someone who was coming to the United States for the first time to attend college. I asked to be allowed to pass through security in order to meet her when she got off the plane. The agent was happy to accommodate us, and when we arrived at the airport, we simply showed our identification and Liz's Normandale acceptance papers and were given a temporary pass through security.

Liz was one of the first passengers off the plane. She wore a bulky pink ski jacket, heavy pants, and a black scarf wound tightly around her neck. *It was a cold day*, I thought, *but maybe I had scared her with my talk about Minnesota's cold weather and snow.* She looked more like she was going skiing than to school. Although she had a huge smile on her face and tears in her eyes as we met and hugged, she looked tired. After all, she had been through a lot over the past days and weeks planning for her trip to the United States and leaving Peru—maybe for many years.

On our ride home, she sat in the back seat and talked nonstop about her flight, about Carlos being supportive that she had this opportunity and that her family was happy for her too.

"I'd like to hear more about that," I said. "And you can call Carlos tonight to let him know you arrived safely."

"All the snow. I've never imagined this much snow." Liz laughed as she looked out the window and then back at me.

We arrived at our house and carried all of Liz's things to her room on the first level. "Here's your very own room," I said. As she walked into her bedroom, she noticed immediately that it had ceiling and floor lamps instead of the bare bulb she had in Arequipa. Her mouth dropped.

"Mamita, it is wonderful. It is more than I could imagine!" She hugged me with tears in her eyes. "Please tell me what I should do with my things."

"You can unpack later," I said as I put my arm around her shoulders. "Sami Tholen is coming over for a light lunch. Let's go upstairs and talk."

"Yes, dear Liz," she said, and then she giggled as she opened one of her suitcases. "I have something for Tom that I think he will like, so may I give it to him when we have our lunch?"

"Of course," I answered. "Bring what you have upstairs, and take your time. But first, Liz, I want you to see your baño."

I showed Liz her own bathroom, and I know I was more excited about it than she was. She looked around the room and at the shower space. "Si, it is so very nice, and I so much appreciate this, dear Liz," she said as she hugged me around my waist.

I left her in her new space and went upstairs. Sami arrived and was excited to hear about Liz's arrival. When Liz came upstairs, Sami hugged her tightly.

"Welcome to the US! We've been looking forward to your arrival," Sami said. "You look great. We'll want to hear everything about your trip and about you."

"Yes, Ms. Sami, it is wonderful to see you again too. I remember the last time when you were in Peru and your husband, Dr. Dick, gave me the wonderful medical book about reconstructive surgery that he signed for me. I brought it with me because it is a treasure to me." Sami had been on this journey with Tom and me as we worked on getting Liz to the United States. It was wonderful to see Sami and Liz together.

The table was set for our lunch, and we all gathered in the living room.

"Tom, I have something for you, but I would like you to sit down right here so I can give it to you." Liz winked at me, and I saw an expression on her face I had not seen before. She was confident and behaved as if she were clearly in charge.

"Sure, Liz." Tom laughed. "Should I close my eyes too?"

"Yes, that is good. Close your eyes."

Tom sat in our rocking chair and closed his eyes. Liz put her gift in front of him and said, "Now, Tom, open your eyes."

She presented him with a forty-eight-ounce bottle of Inca Kola. "Oh, Liz, goodness! I've never seen such a big bottle of Inca Kola. And for me? What a wonderful gift. You know I love this stuff, don't you?" We all laughed and applauded Liz's gift.

During lunch, Sami turned to Liz and said, "Dick and I are going to Catholic mass tomorrow for the late Christmas Eve service. Would you like to go with us? It will be at 10:00 p.m. at our church."

"Yes, I would like very much to go to the mass with you and Dr. Dick," Liz said softly as she reached over to touch Sami's hand.

"That's so nice of you, Sami," I said. "We're going to my niece Jenny and her husband Mike's house for Christmas Eve dinner. We can drive Liz to your church around nine thirty, and then you can bring her back here after the service. Will that work?"

We talked for nearly an hour about the holidays and about the brochure of classes that we had obtained from Normandale College.

In the afternoon, Sami and I helped Liz unpack. She was happy and excited, yet tired from the long flight. Sami hugged her goodbye and said that she would see her the next evening.

"Liz, maybe you should lie down and rest for a while," I said.

"I will do that, Mamita," Liz said. She came over and put her arm around me. "I am just so happy to be here with you and to be in your home. I don't know if I can sleep, but I will lie down."

"Well, now this is your home too." I put my arm around her.

"Yes, you say that, but it will take me time. This is just so much to take in all at once," she said softly. "Now come sit next to me for a few minutes, will you please?"

I sat down on the side of her bed. I wanted to hear about the farewell in Lima with her parents. "Liz, tell me about your family coming to the airport to say goodbye to you. What was that like?"

"Well, my mother and my sister Lydia came from Arequipa, and my sister Marianna and my father who both live in Lima came. They all gave me small gifts. My mother cried and asked God to take care of me. She hugged me, as they all did."

"What did Carlos say about them being there?" I asked.

"My uncle—he was very mad that they were there," she said. "He said that they never cared nothing about me but now that I am going to the US, they want to be nice to me so I will send them money. He was angry, but he wanted the time to be nice for me, so he held on to his tongue, as you say." Tears filled her eyes.

I didn't blame Carlos. He knew Liz's story all too well, and I knew he hated Sofia for all that she had inflicted upon Liz as a young girl. "I understand how Carlos felt, Liz, but maybe your parents regretted how they treated you and now they saw you were leaving Peru, maybe for a long time. They wanted to see you. Maybe without saying it, they were asking you to forgive them. Perhaps I'm wrong. I am one who always wants people to get along and try to forgive and move forward," I said.

"Yes, you are right, Mamita," Liz said.

I didn't want her to dwell on what obviously had been an uncomfortable event. "Get some rest," I said. "We will talk more later." I kissed her forehead, and she hugged me.

"Yo te quiero mucho, Mamita. And thank you, and Tom too, for all you are doing for me," she said softly.

I closed the door to her room and went upstairs. We invited Maria Rubin for dinner. I made saltado with chicken, vegetables, rice, and—as always in Peru—topped with a few french fries.

Maria and Liz were thrilled to see each other. They spoke mostly English, but when the conversation was one on one between them, they seemed to wander naturally to Spanish.

The next day was Christmas Eve. In the morning, Liz showed me CDs of classical Peruvian music that she had purchased and brought with her to give as gifts to my family. We spent the day sitting at the table wrapping CDs and talking about my family members she would meet that evening at Jenny and Mike's house.

"I will like to give the CDs to your brother and to your niece," Liz said as she carefully wrapped each gift.

I invited my ninety-six-year-old godmother Dorothy to join us for Christmas Eve. She was my mother's best friend since childhood and lived in a St. Paul nursing home, where Tom and I visited her, took her out for Sunday brunch when she was up for it, and drove her through the neighborhood where she and my mother grew up. For me, time with Dorothy felt a little like being with my mother, who had been deceased for fourteen years. She told the same stories over and over, but I didn't care. I loved hearing them. I had told Liz about my godmother in emails over the past year. She was happy to know that Dorothy was joining us for Christmas Eve and was eager to meet her.

"It is special times to be with the people that you have known all your life," Liz said. "That is the way I felt about my grandmother, Etelvina, who I always thought of as my mother. I was very sad when she died. But what can I do? It was the calling of God, I suppose. But I do miss her, in spite of the sadness that I had in my life during those years."

After we finished wrapping the CDs, Liz took a long shower. I was glad. It was a luxury she lacked in Peru. Afterward, I knocked on her bedroom door.

"Liz," I said, "I noticed that you didn't have any gloves, and I wanted to give you a pair."

"Come in, Mamita." She stood in the bedroom partially dressed but without her slacks. I saw the large, dark-red scar that covered most of her upper left leg. When she saw me looking at it, I quickly looked away.

"It's okay, dear Liz. This is the scar from the fall I had when I was a young girl and fell into the tree." She rubbed her thigh.

"Does it hurt you?" I asked.

"No, it does not hurt now, but it did for a long time. It is a reminder of when I was sad and alone. Now I see the scar and think of what my life has become, without the sadness. And it is because of you, dear Liz," she said softly.

I hugged her. "You deserve a good life, and I'm only glad that Tom and I can help."

Liz finished dressing. She chose the red sweater and black slacks that Sami had bought her and some black heels. She applied eye makeup beautifully, and her hair shone and hung to her shoulders. "What do you think about my hair? Does it look good?" she asked as she looked at herself in the dresser mirror.

"I think your hair looks lovely. If I didn't know better, I'd say you've spent some time as a hairdresser." I smiled and winked at her.

Liz laughed. "Yes, that is right. If we both didn't know it, we would think that was the case. And lucky for the women who did not have to put up with a very unhappy hairdresser!"

We left to pick up Dorothy in St. Paul. It was cold, and we agreed there was more snow this Christmas than we had seen for several years. Dorothy used a walker, but we got her into the car and headed for Jenny's house. Liz asked Dorothy simple questions. She helped her out of the car and, with Tom's help, up the steps into Jenny's home. Jenny and Mike had their first son, Charlie, aged five, and twin boys, Cameron and Teddy, aged eight months. Dorothy loved the twins, and Jenny let her hold them and play with them on the sofa. My brother Mark and his wife Jackie arrived, as well as my cousin JoAnn and her husband Steve. Mike poured drinks while Jenny served appetizers. Liz was meeting my family for the first time, and she fit in well. Everyone talked with her and then to me, saying, "Liz is wonderful, and her English is so good!"

I hadn't been fond of the holidays since both of my parents had died. I learned I wasn't alone in that feeling. But this year was special. My godmother was with me, as well as my wonderful Liz. I felt particularly happy that night, and as Liz would say, I was content.

I was raised Lutheran but when I attended college at the University of Kansas I found that I very much liked courses in philosophy and religion. As a result, my own beliefs were best suited to Judaism. Later, while in nursing school in Kansas City, I studied and became a Reform Jew. My parents weren't happy about my conversion but with time, accepted my decision. Then while living and working in California I met and married Richard, who was Jewish but had no interest in any religion. In those years, as a result, I continued to believe that Judaism was my spiritual home but I rarely attended temple or synagogue and never joined a congregation.

When Richard and I divorced and my mother died soon thereafter, I returned to Minnesota and to conflicted and ambivalent feelings about the Christmas holidays. Although the Christianity in Christmas had no real meaning to me, I found that I especially enjoyed family holiday gatherings, warm fireplaces, eggnog, hanging wreaths and stockings and hosting Christmas dinners. When I met Tom I even took pleasure in attending Christmastime Lutefisk suppers although I couldn't bring myself to eat the entrée. It was not until we retired to New Mexico that I sought out a reform temple that offered me a Jewish community that now fits my values and beliefs.

After dinner, we visited for a while, and then we drove Dorothy to St. Paul and took Liz to attend mass with Sami and Dick. Tom and I returned home around ten thirty, sat in the living room, and enjoyed a glass of wine.

"We'll have a busy week between now and New Year's," I said. "Liz needs to go to the college to meet Mrs. Harris, get registration materials, take placement exams in math and English, and choose her other courses. And all of this by January 6."

Liz arrived home around midnight, and the three of us talked for an hour. "I am not a religious person and don't attend the mass regularly, but it was nice to go to the Christmas Eve mass with Sami and Dick. I have so much to thank God for." Liz put her hands together as if she were praying.

The next week went by quickly, and every day was filled with a purpose. On Monday I took Liz to my office at Ceridian Corporation. An employee who wrote articles for the company newsletter knew about my medical mission work with CSI and about my helping Liz with medical school, and he wanted to interview us. Ceridian had donated to our mission and he had asked me the previous week if he could do a short interview with Liz and me for the in-house company newspaper. I thought it was a good idea. Liz said it was fine but appeared shy talking about herself. It only lasted ten minutes. Also, my colleagues wanted to meet Liz, so this was the day to accomplish both.

Tuesday morning, we went to Normandale College, where Tom had made an appointment for Liz to meet with Antoinette Harris. Afterward, Liz said that Mrs. Harris was kind and had given Liz exams for English and math class placement, telling her to complete them and bring them with her when she returned the following week to register. She also gave Liz the class schedule for the upcoming semester so she could decide what other classes to take.

After Liz's visit with Mrs. Harris, Tom, Liz, and I walked around the buildings of the college. Normandale is a community college that welcomes students from all over Minnesota as well as internationally. It consists of two modern three-story buildings with many open places in the library and cafeteria and student lounge where students study, visit, and mingle. We were impressed with what we saw, including the course syllabus posted outside of many classrooms and the activity calendars for sports and groups such as the Latin American students' meeting whose next topic was "Adapting to Culture in the US."

When we left the college, we drove the route that public buses take from the college to Southdale, the shopping center only a mile from our home. "Liz, this is where the bus picks up students and takes them to the college," Tom said. "Many days Liz or I can take you to school and pick you up. If you finish classes early, you can either study at the college or take the bus here, and then either we will pick you up or you can walk to our house."

"Yes, I can do that," Liz said. "I am used to the buses in Peru, so that is no problem. And if the weather is nice I very much prefer to walk for the exercise."

When we arrived home, Liz began working on the placement exams. I went downstairs and found her sitting at the round table in the family room working on what appeared to be algebra. She was deep into her math problems and did not raise her head. I was amazed at her concentration.

"Liz, do you want some music on?" I asked.

"No, I do not like the distractions. I know that some people like to have the TV on while they study." Liz laughed, put down her pencil, and looked up at me with a big smile. "It does not seem possible to me to study and watch the TV at the same time. Then I would not be studying, would I? I would be watching the TV."

"That's funny. I usually have the TV or the radio on just for the noise, but I can study then too. We learn different habits, don't we?" I said.

"In Peru, the students from the wealthy families watch the television more," she added. "I have a TV now that my uncle gave to me, but for many years I did not have one, and that was fine; I did not need it. Now I watch it for relaxation, but I do not study with the TV on. Besides, medical school means a lot of concentration that is not possible with the TV."

"Are the problems hard or pretty easy?" I asked as I looked at her work and the equations on the paper.

"No, dear Liz, they are not too hard, but they require a lot of thought," she replied. "Like this one here—I will show you. Some of these are the algebra problems, and they are solved like this." Then Liz explained the problem and her solution. I was impressed. I hadn't completed algebra problems since I was in nursing school studying drug dosages. That didn't last long because single-dose medications and vials were developed, which meant no more calculating.

"That looks like it's over my head," I said as I rolled my eyes.

Liz laughed and then said, "Oh no, Mamita, you would understand it easily. And then there are some trig—how do you say—*trigonometría*? These are the problems to solve that deal with the relationships between the sides and the angles of the triangles, just like this one here." She pointed to the problem she was working on.

"Did you take calculus?" I asked, feeling like a fifth grader on this topic.

"In the secondary school, I took the algebra and the trig ... trigonometry," she said slowly and deliberately to be sure to get the pronunciation right. "I took the calculus when I was at the university in Lima. But you know, dear Liz, I like math very much. I have always liked to solve the problems."

*What an interesting conversation*, I thought. Math came hard for me, and I had needed a tutor when I took calculus in college. But here's Liz, with all the problems and discouragements in her life, saying she likes to solve math problems. And she has no doubt that she can solve the problems. I was amazed by her confidence. Medical school and any career in the health professions was certainly about solving problems. I hoped that whatever career she chose, she would approach it with this same can-do attitude.

She was equally at ease in her clothes. Thursday evening was a surprise birthday party for my good friend Tara to be held at a restaurant near our home. Liz was excited to meet more of our friends and asked me to help her decide what to wear.

"Well, you have plenty of new things to choose from. You haven't worn this yellow sweater yet," I said as I held it up on the hanger.

"Yes, that is nice, but I think I will wear the red outfit that Ms. Sami gave me that I wore on Christmas. I like that one very much." She held the red sweater up in front of herself and looked in the mirror.

"Sure, you look great in that," I said. Then, as I looked at her closet, I realized that it was full of new clothes, yet she had been wearing mostly the same two or three outfits for the past few days. I had shown Liz how to operate the washer and dryer, and she used it every other day or so and apparently washed the clothes she wore, but she still chose to wear the same two or three outfits. I laughed to myself, thinking that most any thirty-two-year-old American woman I knew would be changing outfits at least once a day. But Liz simply picked out what she was going to wear and got dressed. There was no fuss.

The following morning, Liz finished her exams and felt as if she had done well. We agreed that we would take them to the college the following Wednesday and Liz would register for classes that began the next Monday. In addition to the required math and English, she planned to register for biology and psychology. Later that morning, the three of us drove to the Minnesota zoo, where we spent most of our time looking at the animals in their outdoor habitats. Liz was like a kid, saying she had read about many of the animals and knew their species names but had never seen them. It continued to be unusually cold, and I was glad Liz had the heavy jacket she had brought from Peru.

Afterward, Liz and I went to Byerlys grocery to buy what she needed to prepare for us her special Peruvian potato and cheese dish.

As we drove to the store, I said, "So what is in *papas de la huanhuan?*"

Liz laughed as I pronounced each syllable. "Mamita, it is papas a la hu-an-ca-ína. The ingredients include papas, queso, leche, seasonings, soda crackers, huevos, and the yellow *papers.*"

"What are yellow papers, and what do we do with these ingredients?" I asked.

"I will show you. We put everything into your food machine. I think you call it a blending together machine," Liz said.

*Yellow papers*, I thought. What in the world was she making? At Byerlys, I said, "Okay, Liz, it's called a food processor, so tell me what we're looking for and I'll point the way."

"Si, that is good, Mamita. It will be easy to find everything." And it was—we found almost everything with no problem. "Now we just need the yellow *papers.*" Liz looked from right to left.

"I don't know what that is. I don't have any idea what yellow papers are," I said, probably sounding frustrated as well as confused.

"They are here," Liz said, looking up and down each aisle. "I will see them."

"Let's walk around the store until you do," I said. Liz led and I followed with the cart as we went up and down the aisles.

"Here they are," Liz said as she jogged down the produce aisle and stopped in front of yellow peppers. The light bulb went on. *"Peppers!* Of course," I said out loud, feeling silly.

"Yes, that is what I said, Mamita." Liz laughed. "Yellow *papers.* This is what we need."

"Well, it's a matter of pronunciation. This is a yellow *pepper,*" I said as I held one up. "It is spelled p-e-p-p-e-r and pronounced *pepper.* Yellow *paper* is ..." I paused and pulled from my purse a pad of yellow sticky notes. *"This* is yellow *paper.*"

Liz laughed so hard that tears came to her eyes "Oh, Mamita," Liz said. "I am such a silly one. You must have thought, *What is she going to make for Tom and me for dinner using the yellow note papers?* It is so funny.

You can be sure that I will not forget the difference between papers and peppers."

"Nor will I, Liz."

Waiting at the checkout I asked Liz, "What do you think of this store?"

"Well, it is like nothing in Peru, with so much quantity of things and so much to choose from. In Peru we see on the television that in America you have more of everything. In Peru we are too poor to have this much. But tell me please, Mamita, do you think that people really need all of these things, or do they think they need them to be happy?"

"I don't know," I replied, and then I felt sad. Here was Liz from a lifetime of poverty in one of the most exclusive grocery stores in America, and she asked exactly the right question.

When we arrived home, Liz cooked her special *papas a la huancaína*, and I baked chicken breasts. Tom sat at the table and drank a glass of wine as we cooked. We talked about Peruvian food and other favorites that Liz promised to make for us in the coming weeks. Tom reminded us how much he loved the alpaca as I rolled my eyes and wondered aloud how a person could eat those sweet-looking animals. When I served dinner, we slowly enjoyed the labors of our cooking, drank wine, and talked for nearly two hours. It was a wonderful evening. Plans felt like they were falling into place.

## Lomo Saltado – Peruvian Stir-Fried Beef and Potatoes

Normally, you do not find French Fries in a stir-fry, nor do you find rice and potatoes served in the same dish. This Peruvian favorite breaks those rules with great effect. Seasoned with soy sauce and yellow aji peppers, this dish has both Peruvian and Asian flavors in every bite. Using frozen French fries makes this just as great as homemade French fries.

Prep Time: 1 hour; Cook Time: 25 minutes

## Ingredients:

1 pound beef tenderloin or chicken breasts

2 cloves garlic, mashed

2 tablespoons vegetable oil

1/2 teaspoon ground cumin

Kosher salt and pepper to taste

2 red onions, sliced thinly into slivers

1 hot yellow aji pepper, diced

2 tablespoons red wine vinegar

3 tablespoons soy sauce

2 red peppers, sliced into thin strips

Vegetable oil for frying potatoes (optional)

1–1 ½ pounds frozen French fries

2 plum tomatoes, sliced into thin strips

## Directions:

- Cut beef or chicken into thin 1/2 inch strips. Heat vegetable oil in a skillet and sauté garlic with the cumin for 1 minute.
- Add meat and cook on medium high heat until browned on all sides.
- Remove meat from heat and season with kosher salt and pepper. Set aside.
- Add the onions and hot yellow pepper to the same pan and cook 2 to 3 minutes, until the onions are soft, adding a little more vegetable oil if needed.
- Add the vinegar, soy sauce, and red peppers and cook 2 to 3 more minutes. Remove from heat.
- *Optional: If you're making your own potatoes, in a separate pan, fry the potatoes in 1 to 2 inches of oil until golden. Drain on paper towels and season with salt and pepper to taste.*

- Bake the French fries according to directions. Set aside.
- Add the meat to the pan with the onions and peppers. Add the tomatoes and heat for 2 minutes.
- Serve with jasmine rice. Top with a few French fries. Serves 4–6.

Recipe for Lomo Saltado that we ate often in Peru

"Tomorrow is New Year's Eve. How about we go to the Machu Picchu Peruvian restaurant in Minneapolis for dinner and then to the Nicollet Island fireworks?" I suggested. "I bet you'd enjoy that Liz."

"Yes, dear Liz, that sounds wonderful."

Changing the subject, I asked Liz, "When you are finished with your meal, I notice that you always place your knife between the prongs of your fork. Is that a Peruvian custom?"

"Yes. When you put the fork and the knife open on your plate in my country, it means that you would like to have more of the food. When you put the knife in the prongs of the fork, it means you are satisfied."

When I finished my meal, I put my knife in the prongs of the fork. I've done this practice ever since that evening.

"I'll call Machu Picchu Restaurant and make reservations for tomorrow so we get a table around nine o'clock in the evening," Tom said. Then he added, "Liz, do you see fireworks in Peru?"

"Well, yes, there are the fireworks for some of the national holidays and events. It is not as—how do you say—as elaborate as what you have here from what I have seen on the television, but it is what we have. I will like to see the fireworks tomorrow for the New Year's Eve celebration."

On New Year's Eve, we went to Machu Picchu Restaurant for lomo saltado (beef with vegetables and, of course, the handful of french fries). Liz loved the restaurant and talked excitedly with the waiters about Peru and asked them about their lives in Minnesota. After dinner, we went to Nicollet Island and watched the fireworks from outside and when we got cold, from inside an Irish pub. Liz stood next to me with her arm around me and then stood next to Tom with her arm around him. It was the best New Year's Eve I had spent in a long while. We talked about all that had happened that year—the mission to Arequipa, Tom meeting Liz and Carlos, and getting

Liz to the United States. We toasted to the New Year and went home after one o'clock. Liz called Carlos to wish him a happy New Year, and as they talked Liz sounded upbeat. It was a wonderful way to begin 2006.

The following morning, Sami Tholen called early. We hadn't talked since Christmas Eve, and I knew she wanted to hear how Liz was doing. Standing at my desk near the phone, I began telling her about all our activities when Sami interrupted.

"I need to tell you about our Christmas Eve with Liz when we went to mass," Sami said.

"Yes," I replied. "Liz said she enjoyed it very much and that she would like to go with you again."

"Well, yes, we did tell her we would take her to the mass again. But then she told us something that concerns me. Actually, she talked to Dick, and we agreed that you need to hear this," Sami said slowly and then paused.

As I listened to her, I had to sit down

# CHAPTER 27

# Disappointment

It was New Year's Day 2006. I sat at my desk listening to Sami on the other end of the phone. I wasn't prepared for what she told me.

"Dick and I had a nice time with Liz on Christmas Eve," she said. "She talked a lot as we drove back to your house. We were surprised, and bothered, by something she said."

"What troubled you?" Instantly I felt a sense of foreboding. I leaned forward almost as if to be sure I heard correctly.

"She asked Dick if she could visit his office to observe surgeries. Dick said he'd be glad to have her see a surgery. Then I asked if she was looking forward to starting school at Normandale. She said she was but added that she really wanted to be a doctor, that she has dreamed of being a doctor all of her life, and that it is the only thing she has ever wanted." Sami paused.

"I'm stunned," I said. "We've had many conversations about what Liz can study in the US *right now*. I thought she had accepted the idea of being a nurse or a nurse practitioner here. World Education Services needs to evaluate her Peru college work before any other decisions can be made."

"I know this isn't what you expected," Sami said slowly, "but Dick and I agreed you should know."

"You're right," I replied. "Although Liz says she's looking forward to school here, I've noticed that lately she becomes quiet when the topic is discussed. Tom and I need to talk with her right away. If she's got second thoughts, we need to know now." I shut my eyes as I imagined the conversation. I thanked Sami, and we ended the conversation.

I put down the phone and found Tom in the kitchen. He could see that I was shaken. Then I told him what Sami had said.

"This is serious." Tom put his arm around my shoulders. "Was she so taken with the thought of coming to the US and not disappointing us that she went along with the plan in order to be with you?" he asked.

"I don't know, but it doesn't feel good." I sat at the kitchen table shaking my head. "Liz is in her room reading. I'll ask her to come up and talk with us."

Liz came up the stairway quietly, walked across the living room, and sank slowly onto the sofa. "Liz," I began, "Sami told me about your conversation with Dick and her after mass on Christmas. Let's talk about it." I spoke softly although I felt it hard to hide my disappointment.

Liz lowered her head and avoided eye contact, a behavior I had seen before when she was sad, embarrassed, or had bad news. Then tears came to her eyes. Tom and I were quiet. Liz spoke first, without raising her head. I knew what was coming; I could feel it.

The words came out, slowly and deliberately. "Dear … Mamita, I … am … so … very … sorry. I … do … not … know … where … to … start."

"You don't want to go to school at Normandale College, do you?" I asked.

Liz cried so hard that she could hardly speak. "Liz," I said softly, "Sami told me you still want to be a doctor."

"Liz," Tom began, "when we talked about the opportunities you would have here, we explained that although your schooling in Peru will be evaluated by WES, we agreed you could become a registered nurse at Normandale, and afterward you might want to become a nurse practitioner or a biologist. We also discussed and agreed that considering your age and not having a bachelor's degree, acceptance into a US medical school was unlikely."

Liz knew what she was giving up in exchange for a better quality of life. At least she had convinced us that she knew and that she wanted the better life. Now I felt my heart sink in my chest.

"Yes," she managed between her sobs, "I do understand that, dear Tom, and you are right." She continued to cry, barely able to speak. "You have done so much for me, and I am feeling so sad now."

"Tell us what you're feeling," I said.

"Dear Mamita, all of my life I have dreamed to be a doctor, to be able to help the people of my country. It is a dream I have held in my heart since I was a young girl. It is all I have ever wanted. Now I know I could have a better life here and do some other profession in the medical area. But now I do not know what to do."

As I listened, all I could think about was the young girl from Aplao who carried with her the experience of the kind Juan Medina who left an impressionable memory on a young mind and a lonely heart. As she spoke, tears welled up in my eyes and my heart pounded in my chest. *What have I done?* I thought.

Tom looked as shaken as I felt. Liz was sobbing hard, and we knew this was not the time for a rational conversation.

I walked to the couch, sat next to her, put my arm around her, and gave her several tissues. She accepted the tissues and turned her head into my shoulder, continuing to sob.

"I am so sorry, Mamita. I am so very sorry," she repeated over and over.

"It's not your fault." I held her and rubbed her shoulder for what seemed like a long time.

"I would like to go to my room now, please." She looked up at me and rubbed her nose with the tissues, her eyes swollen and red.

"We'll talk later," I said. "Shut your door and lie down if you want to."

"Thank you, Mamita." She walked slowly, head down, toward the stairway that led downstairs to the room I had so lovingly prepared for her.

Tom and I sat silently in the living room. We were both shocked. Tom was more than disappointed; he was angry. I was exhausted and crushed.

After a few minutes, he shook his head and said, "How did we get this so wrong? What didn't Liz understand about what coming here meant?"

"I don't know, but we absolutely *did* get it wrong," I replied. "I got it wrong. It isn't Liz's fault. You can see how much this is ripping her up. She wanted to please us."

"You're right," Tom said. "I remember what Peggy Fairbourne told you before your first Peru mission—and what Maria has told us. Part of the culture of poverty is wanting to please. People tell you not what is, but what they think you want to hear."

"Liz thought we wanted her to come to the US to study. And she was right." I stood up, walked to the kitchen, poured us soft drinks, and kept talking, "I *did* want her to come to the US, not only to study, but to escape her pathetic poverty!" By now I realized I was talking louder than I needed to.

"I hear you," Tom replied. I got caught up in it too."

"But living in or out of poverty isn't important to her," I said, my voice shaking. "She *could* have a better life here, but what Liz defines as better is not what we think is better. I keep hearing Liz say, 'I am content,' and as hard as it is for me to understand, Liz *is* content!" Now I reached for the tissues. "Even going downstairs in her apartment building to use the baño." I still couldn't get the bathroom issue out of my mind.

I kept thinking, *What have I done? This isn't about Liz and her living in poverty. It's about me and what I wanted.*

Tom nodded. "I guess if there's a good part of this, it's that we learned it just before we paid $2,600 for tuition and books at Normandale. I wonder if she would have brought this up if you hadn't told her what Sami said."

"But she did bring it up," I said sadly. "By telling Dick, she told us. I think she knew Sami would share the conversation. It was too hard for her to tell us herself."

Later, as I made dinner, I reminisced about the previous six months. Since returning from Peru in June, I had been consumed with doing what needed to happen to get Liz to the United States. I was sure she'd love it and want to stay. I was wrong. Liz and I had a bond, one that filled both our needs. She desperately needed a mother figure, and I wanted to fill that role. Perhaps that was because, although most of my childhood dreams had come true, I had wanted to study medicine but was persuaded and settled for a nursing career. While my career was successful, I did settle. Liz did not want to settle for any outcome except to fulfill her dream to be a doctor. In addition to my wanting Liz out of poverty, I was also wanting to fulfill *my* dream for her to become a doctor. Perhaps I saw a cause and wanted to help make another young girl's dream come true when mine didn't happen. Perhaps Liz succumbed to the need to be close to a mother figure—and the need to please me.

I tried to understand why she preferred being in Peru to study medicine rather than staying in the United States where she could find a well-paying profession. I kept returning to the truth. Liz and I loved each other like a mother and daughter, like two colleagues and two best friends. Yet, between our worlds, we were much more than a hemisphere apart.

During dinner, the three of us were polite but quiet. We all knew we had to have the tough conversation. Tom put down his utensils. I laid my knife through the prongs of the fork, indicating that I had enough. Liz followed suit.

"What do you want?" Tom asked.

"Well, dear Tom, I appreciate all you are doing for me," she said without the red eyes. "But in my heart, I want to complete medical school. I will have to figure out a way, but I know that is what I need to do."

"I have to ask you, why did you agree to come and let us go through all the steps to get you here if you didn't intend to stay?" Tom asked.

"I thought perhaps I would feel different when I was here," she told him. "I wanted to be here with you who have given me so much."

"We had hours of phone conversation about what it would mean for you to come to the US," he reminded her, his voice firm. "What wasn't clear?"

"I was very confused." She bowed her head. "I know that I could have a better life here, but not being able to become a doctor—well, it is my dream."

"Liz," I said, "we're surprised and disappointed. Tom and I need to talk about this, and then the three of us need to plan and decide when you should return to Peru. I think we're all tired. Let's talk tomorrow."

She went to her room and shut the door, and I fought the temptation to follow her. A while later I saw the telephone light up and supposed she had called Carlos. I was eager to hear what transpired during that conversation. Around eleven o'clock, I went to her room and knocked.

"Are you okay?" I asked.

"Yes, Mamita," she answered in her small voice. "I am fine."

"Do you need anything, or do you want to talk?"

"No, thank you. I need to be alone now."

"All right. I'll see you in the morning." I stood outside her door for a moment. Her lights were off. I thought she must be confused and maybe homesick.

Tom and I talked late into the night. We had questions to answer and issues to resolve. Tom particularly was upset because he thought Liz had lied to us. But I thought it was about Liz being caught up in a romantic idea of coming to the United States. She convinced us probably because she had convinced herself that she understood what leaving Peru meant.

"When I think about it," Tom said, pacing, "she didn't bring the camera we gave her. She brought her computer but only a couple of books, and books are her most important possessions. She knew deep down she wasn't going to stay."

"I know," I told him. "Come, let's sit down and talk about this. We need to focus on what we do from here. I'm disappointed. I'm heartbroken. I had hoped ..." I paused. "But I can't desert her now. She has completed two years of medical school, and in March she will have three years and an internship left. Let's figure out the costs for four more years."

We agreed that we'd support Liz's medical education, but we also wanted more accountability. Her course grades ranged from twelve to fifteen on a scale where twenty is the highest. We thought she could do better and would need to in order to survive the demands that lay ahead. We agreed that Liz needed to commit to working harder.

We also crunched the numbers. The cost to support her in medical school in Peru, including basic living costs, books, and school supplies, would be about $5,000 a year, considerably less than the costs for her at Normandale or any other college in the Twin Cities.

"I also want her to move to an apartment closer to campus where she can walk to school and have her own bathroom," I said. "I think the cost is about two hundred dollars a month. I want to add that to the money I give her."

"That's your decision," Tom said. "You also need to think about your own risk. If she doesn't make the grades or can't handle the demands placed on medical students, can you deal with that?"

"I'll have to. I am too invested in Liz now, and I don't mean monetarily."

"I know what you mean," Tom said.

I thought about what Tom said. What *if* Liz couldn't do it? What if she failed? Would she be back to tutoring students in biology or English at three dollars an hour, *if* she could find work? If that happened, would Liz and I no longer be part of each other's lives? I realized the uncertainties of what may lie ahead. I felt sick. I had no plan B.

The following day was stressful. Although we were all polite, we were also clearly sad. We had invited Maria Rubin to come for dinner, and when she arrived she saw that something was wrong. Tom and I explained what had happened. Maria was visibly upset.

"What is she thinking?" Maria demanded. "She has an opportunity that any poor Peruvian would jump at. I need to talk with her." Maria, after all, had been born and had grown up in Peru and understood the culture more than any of us.

She shook her head and walked downstairs to Liz's bedroom. Tom and I didn't follow, wanting to give them time together. We could not help hearing Maria speaking loudly to, actually yelling at, Liz in Spanish. After a few minutes, I walked downstairs.

Liz was calmly explaining in Spanish what she had told us. In front of Liz and me, Maria started to speak, now in English. "I told Liz she is throwing away the best opportunity she would ever have, to live in the US, to study here, and eventually have a good career with a good income and be out of poverty. I told her she is making the biggest mistake of her life." Liz was sitting on her bed, but she was not crying. Maria and I stood in her bedroom. I didn't know what to say. But Maria did. "Do you understand all the work that Tom and Liz did to bring you here? You need to reconsider this, Liz. You need to consider what your life can become by living and studying in the US."

"Thank you, Maria," I said softly. "I know how well you understand, but we want Liz to make her decision."

"Yes, Mamita," Liz said sadly as she looked at her hands folded in her lap.

I went over to her, sat on the edge of the bed, and put my arm around her. "Dinner will be ready in a half hour. You come up, and we'll have a glass of wine before dinner. Is that okay?"

Liz nodded. Maria and I went upstairs.

"When you were talking with Liz in Spanish, and rather harshly too, I noticed that she didn't cry," I said curiously. "She seemed to defend her decision. When Tom and I talked with her, she was so emotional and sobbed. She could barely speak"

"That's because she sees me as another Peruvian and a peer but not an authority figure. She sees you and Tom as her parents, and she is the child. You are the authority, and she has disappointed you," Maria said.

"I understand," I said. "Now the conversation with Carlos makes sense too. Before you came, Liz told Tom she had called Carlos and explained the change in plans. She said he was very unhappy and had very harsh words for her. He told her she was making a big mistake and that she should not expect us to continue to help her."

Maria was right. Tom and I and Carlos were authority figures to Liz, and with Tom and me she was a child disappointing her parents.

After Maria left, I was exhausted and on an emotional roller coaster. I stood in my bathroom, looked at myself in the mirror, and sobbed. I had to face the truth. I'd pushed the envelope on this one. I took a deep breath and said aloud, "This was just not meant to be. Liz needs to be in medical school in Peru." I realized there were great differences in Liz's and my world, and greater still were the differences in our expectations. My expectations for her were not the expectations of the life she imagined for herself. I had to accept that and accept it now.

The following morning we talked over breakfast and coffee. "Tom and I talked about how we will help you," I said. "We will continue to pay for medical school. You have a good start, Liz, but you have the three hardest years of study ahead of you."

"We also expect you to commit to working harder to bring your grades up," Tom added. "Can you improve your grades?"

"Yes, dear Tom," Liz replied. "I know that my study habits are improving since I have been in school full time for the last year. Also, there are more study groups on campus that are there to help students with tests and assignments."

"Also, Liz," Tom said, "Antoinette Harris went out of her way to help you get accepted at Normandale. You need to meet with her today, tell her you are not planning to register, and thank her for her efforts."

"Yes, I will do that."

"I'd also like you to rent another apartment," I said, "one with a kitchen and bathroom. Can you find something close to campus so you can walk to school and not take a bus and get robbed as you did when your cell phone and purse were stolen?"

"That would be very nice, Mamita. Carlos will understand, I am sure of it." Liz put her napkin next to her plate.

We went to Normandale where Liz met with Antoinette Harris, alone and for a long time. She came out of her office looking sad but smiled and said Mrs. Harris was kind and understanding.

That evening the three of us talked about when Liz should return to Arequipa. Registration for the next semester was at the end of February, so we agreed that Liz would return to Peru the second week in February. Tom and I said that as long as she was here, we would have a good experience and show Liz as much as we could before she left for Peru.

She spent the next morning at the table in the family room downstairs sketching a drawing with a pencil. I sat down across from her.

"What are you drawing?" I asked. Then I saw it was a sketch of a cat.

"I am drawing a pencil drawing of your *gatito*, Mrs. Mertz," she said slowly.

I walked over to behind her chair. "That is very good, Liz. I knew you liked to draw, and this looks just like Mrs. Mertz." I glanced at our black and white cat sleeping contently on the sofa.

"Are you feeling all right?" I asked and sat across from her. "I mean about our plan for you to stay with us for a few weeks before you go back to Peru."

She put the pencil down. "Yes, Mamita, I am fine with the plan. I am only so very sorry, and I hurt inside because I have let you down." She began to cry, got up from her chair, sat down on the floor, and sobbed at my feet as she clutched my legs. It was heartbreaking. She couldn't stop crying.

I stroked her hair and said, "Liz, it's going to be all right, so please don't cry."

But I was crying too. "Liz," I said, "we're going to get through this together." I helped her up and walked with her to the chair where she had been drawing. I reached out my hand and held hers. "Tom and I agreed that we are going to continue to help and support you. I know now that it is the right thing for you to go back to Peru and study medicine. We need to try to have a good time together now that we have a plan."

"Yes, I know you are right. I will miss you, but I will be fine," she said without conviction.

"You *will* be fine, Liz. You have an amazing future ahead of you in Peru. I will miss you too, but we will always be a part of each other's lives, no matter how many miles are between us. I will always be there for you."

The following day Liz and I went to the Mall of America for lunch and then shopping. Most of the clothes people had given her were winter clothes, and when she returned to Arequipa in February it would be midsummer. I wanted to get her some slacks and blouses that she could wear in her next year of school.

We lunched on Caesar salad, sourdough bread, and white wine. Liz was curious about the platters of food she saw waiters carrying to tables and asked me to describe each entrée as it passed our booth. I explained chicken salad and french dip and Reuben sandwiches.

"We have some dishes similar to these in Peru, but they are made with alpaca. I don't think they would be very popular here, do you think?" Liz said, and we both laughed.

Liz lit up as we talked about the classes she would enroll in for next semester.

"I will take pediatrics, gynecology, Clinical Medicine II, and endocrinology." She explained that endocrinology was very interesting to her but that it was also a difficult class because the professor, Dr. Noriega was very strict and gave heavy assignments.

"I know you were studying with a group of students," I said. "Is that still working well?"

"Well, not always. Some of the medical students become very— how do you say it—competitive. They do not always want to share the knowledge or share the books," she explained between taking small bites of salad.

After lunch we walked around the mall and browsed a couple of stores, but I could tell she was only following where I led. When we stopped at Nordstrom, I asked, "Do you have anything particular that you'd like to shop for?"

"Well, Mamita I think this shopping mall is very nice. It is so large, and it appears that a person could find anything here."

"Yes, that's true. This is the largest shopping mall in the US." As I said it, I saw Liz look down the nearby escalator and scan the masses of people. She was bored. I wasn't surprised. She had no need or desire for anything here.

"I remember you told me about the bookstore that has the medical books in English," she said, her expression finally excited. "Is that store here in this mall?"

"Oh, I remember," I said. "That is the Enrica Fish Medical Bookstore at the University of Minnesota. Would you like to go there?"

"Si, I would like that very much. Please. Let's go." She was already walking toward the down escalator.

We had a lively conversation about books and bookstores in Peru while I drove on one of the coldest and snowiest days in January. I didn't care. We took it slow, and Liz was enjoying herself. So was I.

We arrived at the bookstore, and luckily I found a nearby parking place on a plowed street. Liz and I both wore our boots and trekked through huge snowdrifts on the curb and sidewalk. Once in the store, I turned to her. "Take your time and look around."

"Yes, yes, I see there is so much to choose from. It is so wonderful, Mamita. Yes, I will select carefully." Liz gazed in awe of the many used and new books lined up on countless shelves throughout the store.

Few people were in the store, probably due to the inclement weather and classes being in holiday recess. A helpful clerk recommended several books to us.

I wished I had my camera. Liz was enjoying herself completely. I smiled as I watched her but also became teary eyed. I had not been as content at thirty-three as Liz was that day, thousands of miles away from Peru but looking forward to returning to her passion and not at all concerned about her poverty. It was a bittersweet moment.

After an hour and a half, she selected four books, one for each of the upcoming classes she would take, and I found a good resource text on infectious diseases that she seemed interested in as well. As I paid for the books, I said, "Now we'll have to figure out how to get all these in your suitcases. They weigh a ton!"

"Yes, but they are filled with a ton of the information too, you know," Liz responded and giggled. As we drove back to Edina, she talked nonstop.

"Mamita, our professors in Peru tell us that if we can ever get textbooks in English, that it is very good. Not many of my colleagues at medical school have textbooks in English. I am so very proud and so grateful to you." She leaned over and squeezed my arm while I was driving. I smiled and as we agreed we were both cold, I turned up the heat.

When we arrived home, Tom was reading the paper. "You two have been gone for hours," he said. "Did you leave anything at the Mall of America for the other shoppers?"

"We left everything at the mall," I said as we shed our heavy coats and boots. "We went to Enrica Fish, where Liz got some cool English medical books. She said medical books in English are coveted in Peru."

"Yes, Tom, I will show you," Liz said as she brought out each title and explained which class she would use it for. Afterward, she piled the books in her arms and, barely able to walk, carried them to the stairway where she carefully navigated one step at a time.

Time passed. Dinner was simmering, and Tom and I were enjoying drinks. Liz hadn't joined us, so I went downstairs. Her door was open, and she was lying on her stomach on her bed, deeply engrossed in one of her new books.

"What are you reading?" I asked.

"It is the endocrinology. It is very interesting. Now my eyes are sore from reading for so long." She laughed, rubbed her eyes, and told me more about what she read.

"Well, take a break, and we'll have dinner." I put my arm around her, and we walked together upstairs.

I worked some days in the weeks that followed while Tom took Liz to the Minneapolis Institute of Arts, the science museum, the Underwater Adventures Aquarium, and the Museum of Electricity and Life. On weekends, Liz and I visited with my friends and family, or the three of us went sightseeing or visiting. On one afternoon, Tom took her to JCPenney in the Southdale shopping mall. We wanted to buy her some new slacks and blouses for school that she could wear under her lab coat when she made hospital rounds.

"Look for something that you like and find your sizes," Tom said. She casually looked through several racks of slacks and took two pairs, a black tailored style and a tan cotton and polyester blend.

"These would be very nice, Tom. They are size six, and I am sure they will fit me." She smiled and held them up to Tom.

"Try them on in the fitting room to be sure. I'll wait right here for you."

After a few minutes, Liz came out wearing one of the pairs of slacks. "Yes, they fit fine. They are too long, but I can hem them. I have to do that to all of my pants." Liz laughed as she held the second pair up to herself, the hems lying on the floor.

Tom laughed. "I hear that from my Liz all the time. She has to shorten most of her slacks too."

"That is because we are both of the short type, Tom," Liz said, laughing. "You don't know what that is like, I suppose."

She picked out a few conservative blouses that matched and would be good for classes and at the hospitals.

When they came home that afternoon, Tom said shopping for clothes with Liz was more like shopping for clothes with a teenage boy. She was uninterested. I smiled when he told me about it. It was making perfect sense.

I when I made the flight reservations for Liz to come to the US, I made a round trip ticket because it was less expensive, although we planned not to use the return flight. I called the airline and made the reservation for Liz to return to Arequipa during the second week in February. While she was packing, we realized that she did not have enough room for all of the gifts people had bought or given her. We decided that she would take her books and computer, a new stethoscope I had bought her, the new clothes, and as much as would fit in her suitcase but leave most of the winter clothing behind for me to mail to her.

No one talked about the next time we would see one another. We didn't know when that would be. CSI was focusing its missions in Africa and wasn't planning to return to Peru in the near future. Tom and I said privately that we would see how Liz did and try to visit Arequipa when she was close to graduation. Graduation! We agreed that we wouldn't miss that event, and although we didn't say it, we both hoped that graduation day would come for Liz. There were three years ahead plus a year of internship. I knew a lot could happen. A lot could change.

It was a hard day for all of us when she left. We were quiet on the way to the airport. We hadn't planned this, and I felt empty. I didn't look forward to work, and while my family and friends were supportive, I hoped I wouldn't have to do any explaining for some time.

Liz seemed sad too. I imagined she was still struggling with disappointing us and Carlos, whom she would see soon. I kept my arm around her as we walked through the airport, and she put her arm around my waist. We didn't speak. We didn't need to.

Tom showed the paperwork at the security checkpoint and explained that we were seeing Liz to her plane on her journey back to Peru. The three of us sat and talked quietly while we waited for Liz to board.

"Mamita, I do not know how to thank you for all that you and Tom have done for me," she said. "I am sad to leave, but I will do my best in school, and I will make you proud. I will send you my grades too." She reached out for my hand.

"I know, Liz. We're glad we can help. It has been wonderful to have you with us over these weeks." I put my arm around her shoulders. "We know you'll work hard."

"Send us an email when you arrive in Arequipa," Tom said as he hugged her.

"Si, Papito. I will do that. Now please take very good care of each other." She looked at us both. Our eyes were wet. Liz hugged me hard. Passengers were boarding. As she entered the Jetway she turned, waved to us, smiled, and blew us a kiss as she touched her heart.

Tom and I smiled and waved. I blew her a kiss and put my hand over my heart.

As we drove home, I said what was in my heart. "I'm wishing and hoping for all the best for Liz. I want her to complete medical school. I want her to live the dream she has had all these years. I'll be there for her, every step of the way." Tom squeezed my hand as he drove. "She knows we'll both be here for her," he said.

*She has a fighting chance,* I thought. That was a whole lot more than she started with.

# PART 5

# Her Latin Heart Begins to Sing like a Bird

# CHAPTER 28

# La Taqueria de Carlito

After Liz left, our house felt lonely. Although the plans for her to go to school in the United States hadn't turned out, I knew that she was right about returning to Peru. I felt fortunate that she was part of my life. The next day we received the email we requested:

> I arrived in Lima last night at 11:30 p.m. I want you to know that I am so very grateful with you for the wonderful weeks I had in Minnesota and at the same time I want to apologize again for the bad moments you felt because of me. I want to beg you that you please understand that my only one dream in all my entire life is to become a doctor. Life never gave me nothing until I met you two years ago. And since then my life has changed completely for good.
>
> My Uncle Carlos wasn't very glad to see me. He had tough words for me. He was angry and said that one of us had a chance to release ourselves from poverty and I should have taken it.
>
> My promise with you is to study very hard to get my grades up higher and to succeed at Medical school. I promise I won't disappoint you. You are the only one who has been like a real mother to me. I hope you can forgive me.

I called her. "Tom and I aren't angry," I said. "We're disappointed you decided to return to Peru, but I know it's right for you."

"Thank you, Mamita, for understanding and for always being by my side."

"I am by your side, Liz," I said.

"Liz may be doing the right thing," Tom said one evening. "There's nothing wrong with studying in the US. But when international students finish, too many stay here. It's really better for their countries if they return and serve there."

Only a week later, I received a letter from WES, the organization that had evaluated Liz's college work in Peru to determine how many credits would apply toward college in the United States. To our surprise, WES granted Liz nearly three years of college credit for her studies in Lima and in medical school in Arequipa. We had thought perhaps a year of credits might apply but certainly not three.

"I'm glad WES gave her so many credits. But it doesn't change things," I said.

"You're right," Tom replied. "It only means that she could have left Normandale after a semester and probably transferred to the university to complete a bachelor's degree in nursing or another field. I doubt it would have made admission to a US medical school any more realistic."

"I'm not going to share this with her—at least not right now. She may question her decision to return to Peru. Would you agree?" I said.

"I do."

In the next months, Liz shared the challenges of medical school in emails and telephone conversations. She was now deep into the hardest part of the curriculum. In addition, at times she felt prejudice and discrimination from her professors and classmates. She telephoned late one evening, and I could hardly understand her through her tears.

"I do not understand it ... why the professor was so ... so mean. He gave the tests back to all of the other students, but he said I could not have my test results back."

It hurt me to hear her crying so hard.

"Tell me what happened," I said slowly and calmly.

"We had the test of molecular biology, and I studied very hard and felt like I did good on it. The professor, Dr. Noriega, gave the tests back to all the students in the class so they could see where they made mistakes. He said I passed and did very well, but he would not give me my test back so I could see the mistakes."

"Did you ask him why? What did he say?" I asked. I remembered Tom and I had met Dr. Noriega when we visited the university with Liz in Arequipa. Liz told us then he was strict and did not consider students' requests or opinions.

"He said, 'You do not need the test, and I will not give it back to you!'" Liz shouted.

"That's not right. Can you talk to an adviser or someone and explain what happened?"

"No, there is no one who will do anything about it."

"Then I suggest you go back to him and speak very calmly and confidently," I said. "Don't be emotional or cry. Instead, tell him that you know he gave the other students their tests and that you have the right to have yours returned to you, and you would like it now. Try to speak with him privately and be polite and courteous."

"I will do that, Mamita." The following day Liz approached Dr. Noriega as I suggested. He returned the test to her.

Tom and I speculated about what may have happened.

"Another possibility is that she may have turned in a very good exam," he said. "Dr. Noriega told her she did well. He may have wanted to protect his test by assuring that Liz did not share the results with other students."

"That's a possibility. The important issue is that Liz feels like this was discrimination." Similarly, many students studied in groups and shared textbooks to offset the burden of purchasing expensive texts. Liz told us that some groups did not want her included and that others did not share books or knowledge with her.

"Most of the students are protective of their books and knowledge," she told us.

It made me angry to think she was being discriminated against, but the only thing I could do was coach her to stand up for her rights and be professional. *That's a big job*, I thought. Liz asked for advice often. My role was being a mother to her. To do so and be far away was challenging, but it was rewarding too.

Carlos helped Liz find an apartment close to campus. She described it on the phone, saying she had a small kitchen, a bedroom, and her own bath. Knowing it was important to me, she sent pictures of all the rooms.

"It is small and cozy, but I am happy here and it is close to school, so I do not have to take the bus," she said. I could hear the excitement in her voice.

The cost was about $200 a month, and I was happy to pay for it just to know she didn't have to go outside and downstairs to use a shared bathroom.

Soon thereafter, during a three-way telephone conversation, Tom asked about Carlos.

"He lost his regular job at the bank because they laid people off. They call him occasionally. He is very disappointed because he wants to work," Liz said.

"Carlos told us when we met him last year that he would like to own a small restaurant. Does he still have that interest?"

"Yes, he does, and he had hoped to save the money to do it here in Arequipa, near the university where the prices to rent space are better. He wanted to provide a small restaurant where students and professors could eat healthy meals close to school."

When we hung up, Tom said, "I'd like to find a way to help Carlos. Maybe by helping him, we can help Liz as well."

"Well," I said, "What if we gave Carlos a loan to start his restaurant, and then instead of paying us back each month, he paid Liz's apartment rent?"

I felt excited by the idea of helping this man who had been the only person who cared for Liz since she was sixteen years old.

Conversations continued over the next several weeks. Carlos and Liz wrote a business plan that included start-up costs, equipment, working capital and projected revenue. Tom sent Carlos pictures of Subway and Chipotle food counters and offered them as suggestions for making and serving the food. The concept was to provide fast and fresh Peruvian food with the flavors of saltado, a Peruvian favorite, but in the form of a burrito. We would lend Carlos $10,000 to start and run his small restaurant. He would have a year of grace before he started to pay back the loan. Then, instead of paying us, he would give the money to Liz to cover her apartment rent.

In an email, Carlos wrote:

> First, I want to thank you for the great work you did to improve the business plan ideas that we had. I appreciate your ideas. You are correct, that we do not need a freezer but a refrigerator will be fine because I will buy the food fresh every other day.
>
> There are 12,000 students at the university as well as professors, and there is currently no place for them to eat close to campus. The hours of operation I am proposing would be 8AM to 8 PM, Monday through Saturday, which would cover the daytime students and evening students as well as students who come to study on Saturdays.
>
> I am grateful to you, Liz and Tom, for all the wonderful support you are giving to my niece Elizabeth to complete her medical school. My commitment to you will be to pay to Elizabeth the agreed upon amount of two hundred dollars each month to help cover her rent. I won't fail you. I want to work honestly. At the same time I am open to your suggestions and advice. With warmest regards, Carlos Morales.

We signed an agreement with Carlos, and Liz mailed us his signed copy. If he paid the $200 a month to help cover her apartment, it would take about four years to pay off his debt and that would cover Liz's rent through medical school and her internship.

"I've taken bigger risks," Tom said, "but I'll bet Carlos keeps his side of the bargain. And his payments will be the same amount that you would have given Liz for her rent. This way, hopefully, they'll both benefit."

Carlos opened La Taqueria de Carlito in September 2006. Carlito is the child name for Carlos and apparently what he was called as a child. He bought a press and learned to make his own tortillas. When Liz was able to assist after school and studying, she served customers and helped Carlos manage the restaurant. During a call, she was excited to share the latest photograph they had placed on the largest wall of La Taqueria de Carlito.

"Wait till you see it, Mamita! I am emailing you a picture. It is so wonderful!"

Liz had enlarged a photo of Tom and me to about four feet by four feet, and it hung on the wall of La Taqueria.

"Wow," Tom said when he saw the photo. "We not only own a taqueria in Peru, we have our picture on the wall as well!" Over the years, when this story has had rough times, we look at our picture on the wall of La Taqueria and smile, glad we are part of this journey.

Although the restaurant survived for two years and Carlos was able to make a living and pay Liz's rent because of the long hours he put in, the saltado burritos and salads were never wildly successful. Then, when Carlos's landlord increased the rent sharply, perhaps because he believed Carlos was doing well, sustaining the business became impossible.

"My uncle feels that he cannot afford to keep the business open," Liz said. "He thinks that he will close La Taqueria and put the equipment into storage in Lima until he can have the opportunity to reopen again. The bank in Lima has offered him a position working on loans for customers. He thinks he should do this to make a better income for himself and me. And he will continue to pay my apartment rent."

Tom told Liz that it was Carlos's business and that whatever decisions were made were his and we supported him. To me, Tom said, "I've seen small, struggling mom-and-pop restaurants in Peru, and I thought that Carlos might be able to use some American ideas, like we see at Chipotle, to make his restaurant more efficient. And if he used tortillas to serve the saltado, that would save on dinner and silverware. I didn't want to change Peruvian tastes, but I thought students would accept newer ideas. At one time Carlos asked me what I thought about installing a TV set so the customers could watch the news and sports. I told him to forget it. They'd watch but wouldn't buy more food. I might have been wrong about much of it. Change is hard."

In her fifth of the six years of medical school, Liz's curriculum became more demanding and included daily rounds at the hospitals with professors. Liz's grades rose to 16s and 17s with an occasional 19 and remained there.

Medical students were divided into groups of six, whose task was to work together as a team, completing projects, assignments, and

PowerPoint presentations daily. Liz was assigned to a group with five young men, all from professional families. Over the next two years, she became good friends with Jorge, one of the men in her group. Jorge was ten years younger than she but, like Liz, a serious student. His father was a successful businessman, his mother a teacher, and they were putting two children through medical school. Liz said that she and Jorge often prepared the presentations and spent more time doing library research than the others but weren't resentful.

"I want to do my best because I know it will pay off at the end of school," she said.

Although she met with the hardships of difficult classes, long days, and studying late into the night, she was rewarded with good grades. In addition, her professors at the university and physicians at the hospital began to see her as a serious medical student who went the extra mile. Finally, they began to support and encourage her.

In 2008, her final year of medical school, Sofia called and asked to see her. Liz had not seen her mother for nearly two years.

"The conversations always turn to negative talk," Liz said in a phone conversation. "My mother talks about the past and tells me what a bad girl I was. I do not want to hear that."

"You don't have to if you don't want to," I said. "You're right to stay focused on school. Did she say why she wanted to see you?"

"No, not really, just that she wanted to talk to me. What do you think I should do, Mamita?"

"I think you should try to find time when it works in your schedule and see her. There is always the hope that she will be different this time. You could go for a visit and have a plan that if it turns sour, you leave."

"Thank you, Mamita. I will do that. You are right, I am sure, and if it does not go well, I will leave."

She went to Sofia's house on a Saturday. Her mother talked about her relationship with Mateo, Liz's father. While Liz knew that she was neither planned nor wanted, she was not prepared for what Sofia told her. Liz explained it in an email:

> Days ago finally I had the opportunity to have a
> conversation with my mother about the long time I was

apart from her. She was able to tell me that she never loved my father because he was not a good husband to her. Once she learned she was pregnant with me, she was sad. Because of him, she didn't expect me with love knowing that he did not want to be a father again. So she decided to leave him for that reason. She gave me to my grandmother Etelvina because she had to work so hard for my sister Marianna who was by then three years old. My father never asked for me until I met him when I was seven years old.

I'm trying to understand her as well. My mother was twenty years old when I was born. She was really young; on the other hand, my father was thirty four. He was a man with a double life because he pretended to be a single person when he had a whole family behind him. After he married my mother he introduced her to his children from a previous marriage.

Sometimes I feel very sad because I'd have liked to know that I was conceived in love although things in the real world aren't like this. I can't hide it. It is my reality. I feel better after that conversation and I'm just trying to be happy with my career. I'm sure someday soon the reward will be to meet someone nice whom I'll love as my everything and I'll receive back the same.

My mother apologized for those tough times and said that they were both guilty because they left me. To end this topic, I am forgiving my mother and father. I'm not the one who should judge them.

For the first time, Sofia showed remorse. She admitted to Liz that she had made mistakes and blamed her unhappy marriage for her behavior and decisions during the early part of Liz's life. The conversation with her mother haunted Liz. The emotions and situations of her past came rushing back. She telephoned me sobbing.

"I know this stirs up horrible pain," I said, "but your mother is reaching out to you, Liz, because she has her own pain where this topic is concerned. You are right to forgive her and try to move on."

"Yes, I know, Mamita. You are right. She was trying to ask for forgiveness."

"Forgiving your parents is the beginning of healing. When we carry anger and hatred around with us, it only hurts us, and we can't move forward. Forgiving your parents doesn't mean you forget. I'm sure you can't forget, but you *can* move on and, as you say, look forward to your career and your future. Look at what you are doing! Look how far you have come. You are only a semester away from finishing this final year of medical school. You are no longer the little girl from Aplao. You are strong, confident, and soon to be a doctor." I hoped I was saying the right things.

She tried to laugh between her tears. I could tell she was trying to smile. "It was a shock, but I will be fine."

Near the end of 2008 and the end of her medical school academic curriculum, Liz had the greatest challenge of her medical education still ahead of her—the internship. As we corresponded nearly every week by phone or email, I could hear a new confidence and maturity in her words. The third week of December was the graduation celebrating the completion of her academic work and the beginning of her internship. Liz wrote,

> I remember when I was in Minnesota and when I left to return to Peru we were all sad. I was particularly sad because I felt I was leaving the only person in the world who really loved me. I know I made a sacrifice and exchanged the opportunity to have a better life for fulfilling my dream to become a doctor. And now because of your commitment to me and my commitment to study hard, my dream is beginning to come true. Isn't it amazing?

# CHAPTER 29

# Awakening

Between 2006 and 2008, Tom and I talked about where and how we wanted to retire. While our roots were in Minnesota, we agreed our house in Edina was too big for us, and like many of our friends we were finished with shoveling snow, raking leaves, and yard work. The Twin Cities, with three million–plus people, offered much that we enjoyed, including golf, Minnesota Opera, and the St. Paul Chamber Orchestra. But these enjoyments came with traffic, sprawl, and congestion. Tom had retired from his career in development and fund-raising, and Ceridian was agreeable to my staying on in corporate compliance and allowed me to work from home.

Tom was an experienced sailor, and at one time we had contemplated buying a boat for Florida winters. But I had by that time a number of skin cancers, and so much time outdoors became impossible. We had friends who had moved to New Mexico, where they'd built a new home in the Sandia Mountains near Albuquerque. We visited them and began to consider New Mexico, but Albuquerque and Santa Fe, as lovely as they are, experience real winter, meaning snow and cold. As we researched further, Las Cruces, New Mexico, became a possibility. Its population of about one hundred thousand meant less traffic and the feel of a smaller community. Las Cruces is home to New Mexico State University, usually a sign of a diverse and active community, and it boasted of year-round golf and great southwestern food. The idea of enjoying three hundred thirty days a year of sunshine appealed to both of us, and a somewhat lower cost of living was attractive as well. Tom had long talked about building a green home to include solar energy and other energy-saving features.

We started to work with a builder to build a mostly green home in the Land of Enchantment. We spent much of 2007 and 2008 making decisions about our new house and selling our Edina home.

We scheduled an estate sale, and I was surprised at how easy it was to let go of material possessions. Early on the first day of the sale, a woman about thirty-five years old came to look at the piano that had been my mother's.

"My daughter is twelve and is begging my husband and me to buy a piano. I haven't played in years but would be so thrilled to do so again. We just moved into a house where I have the room for a piano," she said as she delicately touched the keys on my piano.

"The piano has a similar story in our family," I said. "My mother played all of her life, and I learned when I was eight. Please sit down. Take your time. I'll be in the other room."

A few minutes later, the woman said, almost shouting, "I want it! It's perfect for our family." Then she turned to me and touched my hand. "Your piano will have a wonderful home with us. We live in Edina too, so it won't be moving far."

We made arrangements for her mover to pick up the piano the following day. I sat down on the bench and could almost hear my mother: *When you get settled in New Mexico, I want you to buy that Baby Grand you've always wanted. Do that!* Maybe, I thought. We'll see. For now I am content.

When the sale was over, I sat in the dark in the living room, drinking a glass of wine and enjoying the moonlight as it reflected off the pond. As my eyes grew accustomed to the darkness, I began to see the near-empty living and dining rooms, previously filled with our possessions of many years. Now there was nothing on the walls, no rugs, and an empty kitchen. *How did I get so much stuff?* I thought. *And why did I think I needed it?* I felt empowered. I felt lighter as I freed myself from the material possessions that had brought me little. I had memories and stories. I had Tom and my brother and my niece. I had cousins and wonderful friends. And I had Liz, a poor girl with sad eyes from a town in another hemisphere, a town that I had never heard of and could not pronounce a few years ago, a girl who had taught me what it meant to be content. I looked at my watch. It was seven thirty daylight saving time in Minnesota and eight thirty in Arequipa. *I have to call Liz … and thank her,* I thought.

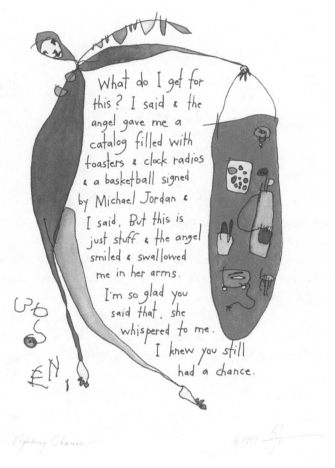

Fighting Chance ; Brian Andrias

What do I get for this? I said & the angel gave me a catalog filled with toasters & clock radios & a basketball signed by Michael Jordan & I said, But this is just stuff & the angel smiled & swallowed me in her arms. I'm so glad you said that, she whispered to me. I knew you still had a chance.

—StoryPeople, "Fighting Chance"

# CHAPTER 30

# Intern

November 18, 2008, was more than just an ordinary spring day in Arequipa. For Liz, it was the day she completed medical school. Tom and I called to discuss attending her academic graduation. "I know it is complicated and expensive to come to Peru," she said. "The bigger day for me would be to have you and Papito Tom by my side at the final graduation ceremony in January 2010. Then I will have completed the internship! It is the major ceremony and a more important day to me."

"That sounds great, Liz," I agreed. "We won't miss celebrating your final graduation with you. Carlos will be there also, is that correct?"

"Yes, of course. He is always by my side for important days."

Liz participated in the formal ceremony on the eighteenth and wore the royal blue cap and gown, the color of the university. She celebrated with her classmates, and of course Carlos took pictures. She called us afterward. "Can you believe it, Mamita?" She was so giddy I could hardly understand her. "Isn't it amazing?"

"It is wonderful, Liz, but we don't think so amazing. We knew you would do it. You worked hard for this day, and you deserve it. We are so proud of you!

"Was anyone else there for you? Any other family, or do you have friends or a boyfriend who was there?" It had been a while since I asked Liz if she had a boyfriend. In the past she said she was friends with boys in her class but nothing serious. She always said, "Love can wait." I was glad to hear that since she had a lot ahead of her with the internship, and I hoped she would not be distracted.

"I met a man, James, online, and we have talked many times over the past six months," Liz said.

"Okay," I said. "Where is he from, and what are his plans?"

"He lives in Maple Grove, Minnesota. He is nice. He went to college in Minnesota and works as an accountant. We had many conversations on the email. Last time I had time off he bought a flight to come and visit me." That sounded more serious than I had wished.

"Liz," I said, "be careful when you meet people online. I wish you had told me about this before, but it's okay." I wasn't sure if I meant what I said, but I didn't want to upset Liz. And more important, she was an adult. "Stay focused on your upcoming internship."

"Yes, dear Liz, I know you are right, and I will put all my energy to do the internship, and then I will actually be a doctor and can practice medicine. Then you and Tom can come to Peru for that celebration."

I gave no more thought to the man she met online. "Of course we'll come to your final graduation," I said.

Following her academic graduation, Liz prepared for her internship.

During the final months of medical school, the soon-to-be doctors took exams that placed them in a Peruvian hospital or private clinic for the year-long internship. Lima, Peru's largest city, has a population of over seven million, a third of the country. Many students apply for an internship at Lima hospitals or clinics for this reason, but few are accepted due to the large number of applications from students throughout Peru. Interns are paid no salary but must continue to pay tuition.

In her last year of medical school, Liz attended conferences in Lima and used these opportunities to network in hope of acquiring an internship at a hospital or clinic. Tom and I encouraged her to look for an internship there because it would offer an interesting and complete experience. Meanwhile, Carlos spoke with military officials he knew at the Hospital de la Policía in Arequipa. Peru's police hospitals serve those whose families work for any level of government. They are well-regarded facilities and operate as full-service hospitals. The plan was a good one, we thought, in the event that Liz wasn't accepted into a program in Lima.

During the last week in December 2008, Liz learned that she and five other students, all men, were accepted at the Police Hospital in Arequipa. Beginning January 1, the six interns would each complete three-month rotations in internal medicine, surgery, gynecology, and pediatrics. Liz admitted to us that she was nervous. I wasn't surprised. Over the years, I had learned that change usually caused her great anxiety. We talked about her anxiety, and once again my role became her coach. "You can do this, Liz," I said, because I knew it was true.

Liz loved the academic part of medical school, and I had known for a long while that she could be a lifelong student. The internship meant more responsibility and more independent thinking. As an intern, while working with professors and the chiefs of the various specialties, she would be assigned her own patients—something she looked forward to. Patient contact, she often told me, was the best part of being a doctor. At the same time, I heard apprehension in her voice at the thought of managing patients, being the only intern on the night shift, and covering for the emergency department of the hospital. I knew from my own experience working with young doctors while I was in nursing school that the intern year could be brutal. Being the low woman on the totem pole usually meant receiving little respect from seasoned physicians. It was a training period and rite of passage, dues to pay.

During the first week of her Police Hospital internship, Liz called. "I have great news Mamita. I have been accepted at the Good Hope Clinic in Lima! Isn't it wonderful?"

The Good Hope Clinic is a private and prestigious clinic located in Miraflores, an affluent Lima district. I learned that private clinics were located primarily in Lima and, unlike most of the government-managed hospitals in Peru, these facilities were privately supported and possessed state-of-the-art equipment. I checked the website and was impressed to see a modern and beautifully furnished facility.

"That's great news," I said. "But can you just leave your internship at the Police Hospital?"

"Yes, I spoke with Dr. Del Castillo, the director of the hospital and chief of surgery, and he will excuse me so I can go to Lima," she said. "I need to leave tomorrow in order to begin the internship next week and not miss any days."

"Congratulations. We're happy for you." I was thrilled at the news. "Where will you stay? Is there someplace close to the clinic where you will live?"

"Yes, Mamita. There are small apartments near there where interns and other doctors live for short periods. It will serve my needs. My uncle is living in Arequipa and has been taking part-time jobs since he had to close the restaurant. He has continued to pay for my rent as he promised, and he will pay for this rent in Lima."

"Okay, that's wonderful. Let us know when you arrive." I knew the twelve-hour bus ride covering nearly five hundred miles was the method of travel she would take. She didn't consider the bus trip a hazard or an inconvenience. We talked about money, and she assured me that she had enough left from the money I had wired to her for the internship tuition, which was the same as the previous year's academic tuition. *Not surprising*, I thought. Although she was not attending the university, the hospitals and the university had an arrangement. The students were required to still pay the regular tuition fee, and the university paid the hospital some of this fee to host the interns. But I knew this was done in the United States as well. Tom and I were thrilled with this good news.

"This is a wonderful opportunity for Liz," I said. "She'll be in a good area of Lima and exposed to higher medical standards than she has been used to in Arequipa." I wondered however, why Liz had been accepted at the Good Hope Clinic in Lima while the five young men in her group of six, all from successful families, were selected for the Police Hospital in Arequipa. Still, I was glad with what I was hearing, so I didn't give it more thought.

During the first week of her internship at the clinic, I didn't hear from her until the end of the week when she emailed that she was having flashbacks of her unhappy years as a young girl in Lima. Liz said she had suffered an asthma attack and was hospitalized in the clinic where she worked, was too ill to work, and thus missed shifts. On a Saturday morning in January 2009, one year from the time when she should finish her internship, I called her.

"Mamita, I cannot go on at the Good Hope Clinic," she told me. "I am the only intern on the night shift, and it has been very stressful for me. I became very sick with the asthma attack. "

"Do you think you had the attack because of the stress of the internship or because you were reminded of your years living in Lima as a young girl? Let's talk about it before you make a decision that could affect your internship and your career."

I thought I probably sounded like an academic counselor. I wanted to be a mother, a friend, and a coach, and I didn't want Liz to make a mistake she would regret.

Tom felt even more strongly than I did about Liz not quitting without trying to work it out with the clinic director.

"Whatever you do, Liz don't quit," Tom said. "Think it through. Try to have a conversation with the director of the clinic on Monday. This is too important. You need to give it another chance." Silence.

Then she said, "I already told the director that I cannot go on, that I will resign from the intern position."

"Can you meet with the director again on Monday?" I asked. "This is critical. Please think it through carefully." I felt helpless but also confused and just a bit suspicious. Why had she been out of communication for nearly a week?

"I need to go back to Arequipa," she said. "My uncle has talked to the Police Hospital there, and Dr. Del Castillo will meet with me to discuss coming back to do the internship. I know how disappointed you are in me, dear Mamita. I feel I am letting you down again." Now she was crying.

"This isn't about letting *me* down," I told her. "It's about making sure you think this decision through. When things don't work out in life, it doesn't mean you have to throw in the towel and quit. We have to be smart and try to stay the course."

We continued to talk, and while I tried to reassure her that I understood how frightening and serious an asthma attack was, I hoped she understood the potential ramifications of her decision. I was both disappointed and concerned. How would returning to Arequipa affect her completing medical school? What if the director at the Police Hospital didn't accept her back? What then? I didn't know. I was mostly concerned that she had made up her mind and quit the internship in Lima before she called us and discussed it. Perhaps she knew that we would encourage her to work it out.

She said she planned to leave Lima by bus that evening. The next afternoon, she would meet with the director at the Police Hospital.

It was mid-January, and we were settled in our home in Las Cruces. I sat at my desk and shook my head. I was disappointed, partly with myself. *Easy for me to say*, I thought. *"Just pull yourself together, kid. You can do it!"* I had no experience with the kind of miserable childhood that Liz had. I needed to be a mother for Liz, but I had no experience at that either. I decided I needed to be a coach and supportive in the way my parents were supportive of me when I was making tough decisions.

"She should never have quit," Tom said. "She should have tried to work it out with the administrator."

"I agree, but I don't think she can."

On Sunday afternoon, Liz met with the director of the Police Hospital. Dr. César Sapaico Del Castillo was her surgery professor at the university, so he knew Liz. During her academic classes in surgery, Dr. Del Castillo was hard on students but he could also be supportive and helpful. Now he was in a different role. As the primary surgeon and director of the hospital, he had even more power.

"I will accept you back at the hospital, but you have missed fourteen shifts as an intern," he told her sharply. "This means that, at the end of the year, when the other interns graduate, you will need to make up the fourteen shifts before you can present your thesis, receive your grades, and graduate."

"Yes, I understand. I agree that I will do that," she told him. "I am grateful that I can return and do the internship here at your hospital."

Liz began her internal medicine rotation immediately. The next twelve months were challenging, even grueling. Each day began at six thirty with hospital rounds alongside physicians and other interns. Afternoons included working with the physicians at the hospital or in their offices and then returning to the hospital for evening rounds and finishing the day about eight in the evening. Every third day, one or two interns stayed overnight to admit patients and manage emergencies. There were no days off. Often Liz was the only physician covering the ER, just as had been at the Good Hope Clinic in Lima. I wondered how being the only physician on the night shift at the Police Hospital was different than being the only physician at night at the Good Hope Clinic. Maybe she was just more comfortable in Arequipa so I didn't give it more thought. She said she was nervous and apprehensive. It was at this point that I knew our conversations needed to occur more frequently. As a nurse, I had experienced what she was going through. I called her every two or three days to listen to her stories; give advice, which she asked for often; and mostly to be her mamita.

During the first rotation, internal medicine, the hospital staff physicians and nurses were rude and demeaning. They would not call the interns by their names but yelled, "Intern! Intern, come over here! Intern, do this charting! Intern, you must see this patient!"

"I'm not surprised to hear this," I said during a call in February. Actually I chuckled for a moment to myself as her description was all too familiar from my early days of nursing school. "What you describe happens here too. Interns are low on the totem pole. You are a new intern. The doctors and nurses think they can treat you like that. You must be strong. Give them a chance to get to know you, and they'll see how hard you work and what a good doctor you'll be."

"Yes, I do understand," she said. "It is what the others say too, and I can do it. I just need to stay focused on the prize."

I was encouraged by her remark. "Yes. Stay focused. And whatever you do, Liz, when they yell at you, don't cry." I was concerned that when doctors and nurses yelled at her, she was hearing her mother or father or Aunt Camilla.

"Yes, I know this is different. It is part of the training. And the best part of my job is when I see my patients get better and leave the hospital. They say, 'Thank you, Dr. Liz, for helping me feel better.' I know that I am helping to make their health and their life better too."

Liz's second rotation, which began in April, was surgery. For the next three months, she would work closely with Dr. Del Castillo and be his first assistant during surgeries. The first night of that rotation, the six interns, five men and Liz, met with Dr. Del Castillo. He quizzed them on their basic surgical knowledge. Then he asked Liz a direct question, which she answered but apparently not to his satisfaction.

He walked over to her. "You're supposed to know this!" he shouted.

One of the male interns spoke up and explained that it was the middle of the night and they were all exhausted.

"What?" Dr. Del Castillo screamed. "You're tired? I don't care if you're tired! I don't care if you eat or sleep! I don't care anything about you. You mean nothing more to me than a fly on the wall!"

The following morning, one of Liz's patients had cellulitis of his leg. She asked Dr. Del Castillo if the patient needed to have the legs cleaned, which she referred to correctly as debridement.

"Of course he needs it! Don't you know anything?" Dr. Del Castillo shouted.

For the next three months, this was the usual daily pattern during surgery and every third evening when Liz did the overnight and covered the emergency department. Her daily interactions with Dr. Del Castillo were mostly unpleasant.

During a cholecystectomy (gallbladder removal), Liz pulled the retractors to separate the incision so Dr. Del Castillo could remove the gall bladder.

"Can't you pull any harder, intern?" he demanded. "How do you expect to have children if you aren't strong enough to pull on these retractors?"

Following surgery, Liz closed the patient's incision.

"Are you done, intern?" Dr. Del Castillo yelled. "Your time is nearly up. We have more patients!" Liz continued to close the incision without comment. Within a few weeks, she began to find humor in some, but not all, of his comments.

"He is a short man, and I and the other interns think he needs to act big to sound important," she said during a phone conversation. Also, as Liz became better acquainted with the nurses, they treated her more respectfully and reassured her that the doctors, particularly Dr. Del Castillo, yelled at all the interns. It wasn't personal.

A few weeks into her surgery rotation, Dr. Del Castillo took Liz aside and told her he had been invited to speak at a conference in Brazil on the treatment of Mirizzi's syndrome, a condition that results in the compression of the common hepatic duct. He said he expected her to do the research for his presentation. Liz tried to reason with him.

"I will try to do this for you, doctor, but I also have to present my thesis topic soon, and between shifts at the hospital I do not know if I will have the time to complete—"

He interrupted her abruptly. "You are smart and strong. I want you to do my research project. I don't care what else you have to do. You must do this. If you don't, you will fail this rotation. It is your decision what you want to do."

"On the one hand, he complimented you," I told her, "but on the other, he is pushing you beyond what you can do."

"But what can I do?" she asked me. "I could do the research by studying medical records of patients with this condition during the nights when I am at the hospital. I have to say that I am exhausted."

At the end of June, Liz was finishing surgery and ready to begin gynecology in July. She finished the presentation for Dr. Del Castillo and also the first draft for her thesis. She was ready to present it to the next jury of physicians. We continued to talk nearly every evening when she was at home.

"I feel so stressed out, Mamita, and so discouraged," she said sadly. "I know this is not what you want to hear, but for the first time, my passion for medicine is dying. My passion and love for humanitarian causes is very much alive, but I am discouraged."

"I understand how you feel," I told her. "You are working long hours, and when the surgeons and particularly Dr. Del Castillo treat you poorly, it is hard to stay positive."

"Do you know what all the interns call Dr. Del Castillo? They call him Dr. J. That stands for *jerk*." Liz laughed, and I took a deep breath. Maybe she was handling this better than I thought.

"I just need to concentrate on doing my best," Liz said, sounding better.

"That's right. And you have only six months to go." She also had fourteen shifts to make up but I decided not to mention that.

Two days later, she received news about her project.

"The thesis has some problems," she said. "Everything was ready to do the survey for the research, and then there was a complication with the survey that I need to conduct on the topic. I am upset because I paid three administrative people to help me. Hours were wasted, and this will increase the budget I had to complete the thesis."

"Don't worry about the budget," I told her. "Just get it completed. I'll wire you more money if you need it. "

"The professor has the power. I am just the student. He will administer the survey next Monday. I asked for special permission from Dr. J to leave the hospital to work on the survey administration with my professor. I was surprised that he was very understanding and said I could do it."

"Well, maybe Dr. J sees how hard you are working," I said.

"Yes, I think you are right, Mamita. I am always at the hospital, and I do my best every day. Some of the other interns leave early or arrive late. It makes me angry that they get by with doing less."

The next day we talked again.

"I have a green light to go ahead with my thesis," she said. "The topic was approved, and the survey will be administered. I am so excited."

"What is the topic?" I asked.

"It is titled *The Relationship between the Epidemiological and Academic Factors Contributing to Symptoms of Depression in Medical Students at the Catholic University of Santa Maria.*"

It wasn't surprising that her topic was depression; Liz had shared with me over the years that she suffered from it periodically. Nor was it surprising considering her experiences. During her clinical rotation in psychiatry, several professors were helpful and good listeners when she asked to talk about her own issues.

"It is good news about the thesis, but I had a terrible day at work. I accidentally broke a table during a surgical procedure. Dr. J yelled at me and told me I would have to replace it before I could finish my internship. I'm telling myself to be patient and be strong, but it really sucks. I have to tell you that I am sick of this. I don't care about the grades now either."

"Try to keep the right perspective," I told her. "You are close to finishing, and you're exhausted."

"There is also an issue with Dr. J and the university. The contract between the hospital and the university is not clear. Dr. J has all the power and is making us work extra hours and do extra shifts. All the interns met with him, and he said, 'If you do not like this, then you are free to leave the Police Hospital and your internship.' Nothing changed. We continue to work from 6:30 a.m. until 7:00 or 8:00 p.m. and then do eight overnight shifts a month."

I worried about Liz and called her often. Sometimes I changed the subject and talked about something fun that Tom and I did, and it seemed to help.

Dr. Del Castillo was Liz's surgery professor at the Catholic university, her "boss" at the hospital, and also a member of the jury of three professors when Liz sat for her upcoming final oral exam.

"The doctors gave me a grade of nineteen when I presented my final oral exam to the jury of physicians. The two other jury members said, "You can go now, Ms. Cardona." But then Dr. Del Castillo said confidently, 'No, I want to ask her one more question, and this one she will fail.' He said it as if he wanted to see me fail. Then he asked me about abdominal trauma. I gave the answer very well, and he congratulated me. I left the room jumping. It was stressful, but I did it," Liz said feeling elated.

At the end of June, she said, "The surgery doctors are treating me with more respect. Now Dr. J is treating me better in front of the medical students from the university he brings to the hospital. He has invited me to his office to meet and talk. It is really funny. One day he yells at us, and the next he is polite and wants our support"

By mid-July, Liz was starting to believe that she would be the doctor she dreamed of. She liked gynecology, and the chiefs of the services treated her well. Her final rotation, pediatrics, started in October. While she found it the least interesting of her rotations, she did well and enjoyed the experience.

During a conversation near the end of November, she said, "Guess who is an inpatient at the Police Hospital? Dr. J! He suffered from a ruptured Achilles tendon from a tennis injury. He had surgery at this hospital, and I was the intern on duty, so it was my job to see him and examine his wound. He treated me so well, Mamita."

"That is amazing, Liz. What did he say?"

"He was very nice and respectful and said 'Hello Dr. Liz,' and he gave me a polite kiss." It is customary in Peru to kiss people on the cheek in both social and professional situations when you meet. She continued, "He congratulated me for the good comments he has heard about my work and said he is very proud of me. Isn't it amazing, Mamita?"

"That's great, Liz," I said. "He has seen how hard you work and what a good doctor you are."

I thought of a film Tom and I had seen recently. In *City of Angels*, Nicolas Cage's character says, "Even in hell, sometimes an angel makes an appearance." Liz's internship was about to come to a close. It had been a hell—that was for sure. But maybe Dr. J wasn't such a bad guy after all.

Liz wrote:

> One of the chief doctors said that when Dr. J sees a very good student, he does not say that the student is doing well. He wants the student to work harder. He is very hard on the student because he expects more out of the best students. He will however be making the decision about whether I have to stay the extra fourteen shifts in January to pay off the days I missed at the beginning of the internship. He is so unpredictable and moody. It is hard to know.
>
> It is amazing how much respect I have gained with the doctors and all of the staff. They all call me Doctor Liz, and my patients call me Dr. Cardona, even though it is not official yet. Dr. J behaved so nice and treated me so good and made me feel like a real professional when I checked on him during the daily rounds after his surgery.

I had good thoughts. Liz had proved herself. The week before Christmas, she told me that she, Carlos, and several of her doctor friends had made baskets and were filling them with food.

"This weekend I do not have to be at the hospital on Saturday. It is so close to the end that the hospital gave us this Saturday off. We are going to bring the baskets of groceries and some clothing too and take them to five families who live in the very poor district far outside of Arequipa."

"What a nice idea," I said. "Will you have a truck or a car?"

"My uncle knows a man who will loan us his truck. We are all working very hard to get as much food and clothing for these families as we can. I want to give back to people, Mamita, like you and Papito Tom have done for me."

I was proud of Liz for many reasons—for what she had accomplished over the past six years, for moving past the sadness of her youth, and for finding her dream and hanging onto it. But I was probably most proud of her for what she wanted to do with her life. She was not impressed with money or material things. Now the poor girl from Aplao, soon to be the doctor she dreamed about, was giving food and clothing to others.

The last week in December, she wrote:

> The internship is nearly coming to an end. I had a disagreement with another intern, but I worked it out and it is ok. I am dealing with people's lives and with their health and well being, so I take my work very serious. I feel so good about what I am doing now. I have had many days that have been very difficult for me. But I thank you for listening and being by my side. Now I am holding my head up and I am proud. I never imagined this could happen to me and it has brought me so much happiness. I know this is just the beginning of something bigger for me. I am excited for my future for it is a future filled with hope.

December 31 arrived, and Liz finished the internship. The following day, she met with Dr. Del Castillo, who was discharged from the hospital but still using crutches. He willingly agreed that Liz had fulfilled her commitment at the Police Hospital and that she was free to file the paperwork necessary to present her thesis. She did not have to complete the additional fourteen shifts. She would graduate on January 28, 2010.

Following her meeting with Dr. Del Castillo on New Year's Day, Liz met with the professors at the hospital, who gave her the grades for her four intern rotations. She called me and was so excited that she could hardly talk.

"Mamita, I got my grades, and I am so excited. Guess what? I got seventeen in surgery and gynecology, nineteen in internal medicine, and twenty in pediatrics! Can you believe it? Isn't it amazing?"

"Liz, that's wonderful! But I'm not surprised. You've worked so hard and been so serious about all of your work. Your good grades are proof that your professors saw that too. Congratulations. We are so proud of you!"

Tom and I were thrilled. Liz had brought her grades up from elevens, twelves, and thirteens to seventeens, nineteens, and even a twenty. She demonstrated an outstanding record in her academic studies.

We rushed to make both airline and hotel reservations. We would again stay at the Casa Andina Hotel in Arequipa. We arranged to leave for Peru on January 23 and planned to spend eight days with Liz and Carlos. It was a bittersweet time for both Liz and me. We had traveled a six-year journey together, and although medical school was completed, both our lives would always be connected. Liz had become the doctor she had dreamed about since she was a young girl, and I saw my priorities more clearly than ever before. I found I could let go of small stuff and big stuff too. Liz had taught me the meaning of being content, and to some extent I learned about being a mother.

She emailed me on New Year's Day 2010:

> The day I met you I did not have any coins in my pocket, or any hope in my heart. I did not know where my life was going to turn. I believe that it was a special meaning that we found each other. Sometimes I do not know how I can thank you for being there for me, for being my mother, for loving me and for caring about my life.
>
> All my life I have thought about what it would be like to be away from the sadness I lived as a young girl. I am a dreamer person. I dreamed to be a doctor but never thought it could happen for me. Now I see that the dream is already in front of my eyes.

# CHAPTER 31

---

# Graduation

I shouldn't have been surprised when she told me that there were final details to register her documents before graduation.

"Okay, Liz, what does *final details* mean?" I asked, knowing full well that Santa Maria University would have a hand, or hands, outstretched.

"Mamita, I hate to have the discussions with you about fees. You have done so much for me all these years."

"Tell me what you need. Send me an email today, and I'll wire money in the morning. Also, do you need a nice outfit for graduation? Tell me so we can get you graduated," I said laughing.

Liz laughed too. "That will be wonderful, Mamita. Thank you so very much for everything. It will be a very special time to have you by my side again."

Liz's fees came to $1,800. I sent $2,500.

We flew from El Paso to Houston and then to Lima. After a layover of several hours in Lima and a final hour-long flight, we arrived in Arequipa at 5:45 a.m. on the twenty-fifth. Our baggage arrived quickly, and as we walked toward the taxis, we saw Liz and Carlos waiting. Liz wore a denim jacket over black slacks. She took my hands into hers and looked hard into my eyes.

"Dear Mamita, it is so amazing to see you." She had tears in her eyes. We hugged hard. Still holding onto my hand, Liz turned to Tom. "And Papito Tom"—more hugs and for Carlos too.

"It's good to see you, Liz. You look wonderful," I said as I ran my hand over her head and smelled her clean hair, still damp from her shower.

With our arms around each other, we all walked to the van that the Casa Andina Hotel had sent to meet us. I noticed that Carlos had tears in his eyes, as did I.

Dog tired, we checked in at the hotel, and the four of us went to the dining room for a breakfast of the scrambled eggs I loved, fruit, and delicious Casa Andina coffee. Tom also chose sliced alpaca, his long-awaited delicacy.

I asked Liz if everything was arranged for Thursday's graduation.

"Yes, the time will be about ten or eleven in the morning. I will know exactly later today," she said. "It has been a crazy last few days getting all my documents in order and having the copies made of my thesis for my professors at the university."

She looked and acted confident, a confidence I hadn't seen before as she held her head high and made good eye contact with Tom, Carlos, and me.

I asked her to tell us about her oral thesis presentation to the jury of physicians. "I know you were nervous, but what was it like?"

"Yes, I did it. I was so nervous. I had to speak about the thesis to the head of psychiatry and two other professors. And it went … *perfect*." She almost squealed as she squeezed my hand.

"Each professor asked me questions. This lasted for about an hour and a half. Then they excused me for about fifteen minutes. That was when I was really worried, Mamita!" Liz laughed, and we saw her beautiful smile. *Oh, how I missed that smile and her laugh.*

"Then they called me back and said, 'Dr. Cardona, that was an excellent presentation. In fact, it was perfect!' They each congratulated me, shook my hand, and hugged me."

"They called you Dr. Cardona!" I said.

Liz paused and looked thoughtful. "Well, apparently, I am a doctor, Mamita!" she said, as if realizing this for the first time.

Tom and I laughed.

"Yes, apparently, you *are* a doctor!" Tom said.

Liz translated for Carlos, who laughed and nodded. "Sí, sí, ella ahora es doctor verdadero! (Yes, yes, she is a real doctor now!)"

Liz blushed. "Well, it is taking me some time to get used to being called doctor. The doctors and nurses at the hospital have been calling me

Dr. Cardona or Dr. Liz for weeks, and sometimes I have to pinch myself to think that this day has really come."

"Your day is here, Liz, and you made it happen. You accomplished this yourself," I said.

As we left the restaurant, we agreed that Tom and I would unpack and rest and that Liz and Carlos would come back to the hotel for dinner and to plan for the week.

When they returned, Liz presented us with a copy of her thesis. "I want you to see the dedication that I wrote," she said as she handed me the one-hundred-fifty-one-page, dark green, eight-and-a-half-inch by twelve-inch bound book. I thought she might give us a copy of her work, but I didn't expect the dedication:

> A mis queridos padrinos quienes siempre me demostraron su amor y dedicación incondicional apoyándome en mis proyectos a seguir (To my dear godparents who have always demonstrated their unconditional love and dedication to support me as I continue my plans)

We were tearful and happy.

At dinner that evening, we talked about what Liz planned to do after graduation.

"I will be moving to Lima. I will look for work in one of the large private clinics there and will find a small apartment." Liz had told me earlier that she did not intend to do the SERUMS. "I need to make an income, Mamita. I cannot go to a remote town or village and spend another year without salary," she said convincingly.

"But if you don't do the SERUMS, you can't work in a public hospital in Peru. In addition, you can't become a practicing physician in any other country or a licensed physician in the US," I said.

"Yes," she answered, "but I have to start to make an income, and there are private clinics and hospitals."

I was frustrated. I knew that during the SERUMS, the new doctors received no income.

"Liz, Tom and I will pay your expenses until you are finished with the SERUMS. I understand that this period is really just nine months. You can do that. It will be over before you know it, and this is a chance to get very good experience before you practice," I said.

"No, I can't do it. I need to start to make money," she replied firmly.

Liz's determination was one of her strengths, and although I was disappointed, I didn't challenge her decision again. I also wondered if returning to a remote community in Peru might remind her too much of her girlhood in Aplao. I knew she had a good head on her shoulders, and after she completed her internship, I hoped she would make good decisions about her future. Still, I had questions.

"When you went to Lima for the short while at the Good Hope Clinic, you were very stressed. Do you think it will be different for you now?" I asked quietly.

"I do, Mamita. I have some contacts in Lima, and I am feeling that it will be a good thing for me now. I am not worried about it at all. You need to believe me," Liz said, looking directly at me.

As we walked from the hotel together, Tom said, "Look, there's Ronald." Tom and Ronald shook hands, and Tom asked him if he remembered us from 2005. Ronald, who spoke better English than I remembered, said he did, although we both thought that unlikely. Tom asked Ronald if he could drive us the next morning to Liz's apartment and then to the hospital where Liz wanted to introduce us to doctors and needed to discuss with them her reference letters. Ronald happily agreed.

We walked a few blocks to the Ary Quepay restaurant on San Francisco Street. As we toasted with wine, Tom said, "Liz, I have to tell you that we are so very happy to see you and to share in this important time in your life. But if Liz and I had to turn around tonight and go back to the US, the trip would have been worthwhile. You look great, and you sound so confident. You have the voice of a woman who knows what she wants to do. We are so very proud of you."

"We know it hasn't been easy," I added, "but you did it! When we met in 2004, I knew you had the strength to make your dream come true." I reached my hand across the table to her.

"Thank you, Mamita and Papito." She squeezed my hand. "We have been a team on this journey. I could never say enough about what you have done for me and for my uncle also."

I had prepared some words that I wanted to say to Carlos. Looking at Liz and then Carlos, I read the words in Spanish. In English, the words said:

> Carlos, Tom and I want to tell you how much we appreciate all you have done for Liz. You have been present in her life through many difficult times and given her the support and love that has helped her. We respect you for the love that you've given her and will always hold you in our hearts.

Carlos wiped his eyes.

"I know too, Mamita, that when I was in Minnesota, it was a very sad time for you," Liz said. "I disappointed you. But I knew I had to be the doctor that I have dreamed of all my life. I thank you so much for staying by me."

Following dinner, as we walked back to the hotel, Liz told me that she had cut all ties with her father. "He only tried to contact me once over the last four years, and when he did, he was always cold and unfriendly. I do not want that in my life."

"Was it hard for you to come to this decision?" I asked.

"No, not really. It is the same with my mother," Liz said. "I called her at the Christmas holiday, but I did not go to see her. I was very polite and wished for her to have a happy Christmas, but I was finishing my internship and moving forward, as you say."

"Does your mother know you are a doctor?" I asked.

"Yes, she does, but she does not ask about me. I am content. Really, I am."

The next morning, Ronald drove Tom and me to Liz's apartment. It was déjà vu for me, I thought, remembering that Ronald was the first cab driver I met on our 2004 mission and he took us to the hospital every day. During those days I was learning the story of the girl from Aplao with the sad eyes while Ronald was cheerful and happy. I never imagined that six years later, I would again be in Peru celebrating Liz's dream and Ronald would be driving us to our destinations. *What a small world*, I thought, *and what a wonderful coincidence.*

When we arrived at Liz's apartment, Tom and I were shocked. At the gated entrance, where a sign read *Encantado* (Enchanted), Ronald said, "Cardona," to the guard and the gate was opened. Liz's apartment was between several condos and single-family homes. Liz, dressed in brown slacks with a white blouse and low-heel shoes, met us at her apartment door, where Ronald said, "Congratulations doctor!"

Liz blushed. "Gracias, Ronald. Thank you."

Her second-floor apartment was an incomparable improvement over the dreary rooms she had lived in on Calle Samuel Velarde. A small kitchenette overlooked other homes. An adjoining sitting area had a nice, floral-patterned upholstered sofa, matching chair, pictures on the wall, and a good-sized mirror. A few steps beyond was Liz's bedroom with a double bed, dresser, and sizable closet. A window let in light and fresh air. The bathroom with toilet, basin, and shower was clean and bright. The apartment was carpeted and furnished, and Carlos paid $200 a month in keeping with our agreement.

"It is small but cozy, Mamita," Liz said proudly as she opened a drawer and removed an envelope. "Sit here." I obeyed. "These are the receipts that show that my uncle has paid for every month of my rent."

I put my arm around Liz. "I know Carlos has kept his word."

Carlos arrived a few minutes later carrying a bag of yogurt, several apples and oranges, and bottled water. He put the yogurt and fruit in Liz's small refrigerator, kissed Liz and me on the cheeks, and shook hands with Tom.

"We should go to the hospital now," Liz announced, sounding a bit like our tour guide.

"We're ready, doctor," Tom said.

Liz blushed and giggled. "Yes, Tom, you are right. Apparently, I'm a doctor."

The six-story Police Hospital, whose lobby proudly displayed a painting of the Virgin Mary, bustled with doctors, nurses, and patients. After going up a short stairway, we arrived at what I imagined was the emergency area. People of all ages, waiting to see a physician, sat on long benches. Mothers held crying babies. Children played catch with a tennis ball. There was a cacophony of voices, and we needed to speak loudly in order to hear one another.

"I am going first to see an orthopedic surgeon about a reference letter," Liz shouted. "Please follow me." Liz led, and Tom, Carlos, and I followed like ducklings. Liz knocked on the door of an examining room.

A male voice said, "Come in."

Liz entered and invited Tom and me in as well. Inside, a doctor was removing a young man's arm cast. He stopped his work, smiled, talked with Liz, and read the paper she put before him. Meanwhile, the patient looked at Tom and me and waved.

"Hola," he said as he smiled.

"Hola," we replied.

I chuckled to myself. What a funny scene this was—outsiders coming into a treatment room while a patient was having a procedure? This casualness would never be allowed in the United States, but they were fine with it here. Bottles of liquids on a mayo stand appeared to be disinfectants. I thought they looked a little scary, with caked fluid around the tops. But I was in Peru. Conditions and expectations were somewhat different. I also reminded myself that, in spite of the conditions that I was used to at home, these patients usually got better and clearly appreciated their care.

Next, Liz led us to surgery, where we encountered Dr. Reyna Medina, the chief of anesthesiology and Liz's anesthesia professor. She hugged Liz and me and shook hands with Tom. Four or five surgical nurses appeared in their surgical garb, and all talked with Liz and offered her their congratulations. After leaving Dr. Medina with the reference request, Liz led us on a thirty-minute walk through the hospital's six floors to show us where she had worked over the past year. "The elevators do not usually work," she said matter-of-factly.

Tom turned to me and whispered, "Are we surprised?" We both laughed, remembering Honorario Delgado hospital on the other side of the city.

Back at the hospital lobby, a slight-framed gentleman who was on crutches and dressed in a striped short-sleeve shirt with a cell phone hanging around his neck caught Liz's eye. She ran over to him, and he kissed her on the cheek as she hugged him. The crutches gave him away. Standing before me was Dr. César Sapaico Del Castillo—or Dr. J, as his students called him—surgeon and director of the Police Hospital. I was not prepared for his graciousness.

After Liz introduced us, I started to speak with him in my limited Spanish, and he turned to me and, in excellent English, said, "It is very good to meet you. Elizabeth was a fine intern, and she will be a wonderful doctor."

After Liz discussed a reference letter with Dr. Del Castillo and we began to leave, he reached to hug me, holding the two crutches with one hand. He looked at me, smiled warmly, and said, "It is wonderful what you did for Elizabeth, and you should be very proud. Enjoy your time in our beautiful country and at the graduation celebration as well."

*Whew!* I thought as I felt speechless for a moment. Here was a man who had been brutal to Liz and, to her, seemed at times just plain mean-spirited. But what the nurses had said about him was undoubtedly true. He was hardest on the interns whom he thought were the best. I was grateful for this small miracle.

When we left the hospital, Ronald drove us to the university, where Liz needed to file still more paperwork.

The Santa Maria University campus was just as I remembered, with students bustling about and mingling in groups. At the medical school office, Liz knocked on the office door of Dr. Jacinta Torres, dean of the medical faculty and her biology, cytology, and histology professor. She had known Liz throughout her medical school classes and been kind and supportive of her hard work from the beginning.

"It is an honor to meet you," she said to Tom and me in Spanish. "Thank you for all you have done for Elizabeth. She has worked very hard and has persevered through her own hardships to meet her goals. She will be a fine doctor. You should be very proud." She hugged me, held onto my arms, and looked deep into my eyes. I welled up with tears, and I think I saw tears in her eyes as well. "It is amazing what you have done for Elizabeth," she said slowly and firmly.

In my best Spanish, I replied, "No, Dr. Torres. Elizabeth did everything. It is an honor to meet you and to thank you for the support you have shown her."

Then Dr. Torres turned to Dr. Cardona. She held her arm and said quietly as she looked into her eyes, "Are you sure, Elizabeth, that you will not do the SERUMS? It is not too late to sign up."

"No," Elizabeth responded. "I will not, and I am sure."

I wasn't sure what that exchange was about. I'd ask Liz later.

At that moment, I had no doubt that Liz would accomplish exactly what she had set out to do. During her internship, I had often thought about the profound impact she had made on my life. I saw her persevere beyond poverty and abuse to reach what was then a dream and now a reality. Although I had tried to explain this to her, I always felt that she didn't entirely understand how much I admired and respected her.

The next morning, Ronald drove us to the university for a mass followed by graduation. During the ride I asked, "Do you have children, Ronald?"

"Si, two daughters. They are eighteen and fourteen. I am very proud of them, like you and Mr. Tom are proud of Dr. Cardona, senora." Ronald looked at me in his rearview mirror and smiled. I felt like a mother hearing the pride another parent had for his children.

It was a warm and sunny summer day. The mass was held in a large conference room. An older woman with a lovely voice sang hymns, served as acolyte, and read the epistle. The priest read the liturgy and homily utterly without feeling and without looking at his congregation. Graduates, parents, relatives, and friends attended. A hymn was sung in Spanish to the tune of "Blowing in the Wind," the song that made Peter, Paul and Mary famous. When the sacrament was offered, no men participated, but many women did.

Following mass, Carlos, Liz, Tom, and I walked to a campus auditorium, where graduating students sat in the first four rows. Instrumental music played through the auditorium's sound system. Proud parents and friends carried flowers and wrapped gifts. People were well dressed—men in suits with ties and women in dresses, some in elegant strapless dresses with high-heeled shoes. We remarked to one another that, unlike in the States, we saw no tattoos. Carlos, Tom, and I found three seats with a good view of the stage. People chattered. I felt certain that Tom and I were the only Americans.

The commencement was scheduled to begin at eleven in the morning, but when the auditorium filled to standing room only, the start was delayed. Suddenly, a familiar song began playing though the sound system. I saw Liz stand up in the first row and look back toward the crowd to find us. Spotting us, she waved, and we waved back. She blew me a kiss and touched her heart as the music played the song written by Jeff Silbar and Larry Henley in 1982, "You Are the Wind beneath My Wings."

For a long moment, my mind flashed back to six years earlier, when I heard for the first time the story of the girl of Aplao, given to her strict grandparents because her mother didn't want her. I saw her in their farmhouse made of clay bricks and with a dirt floor. I chilled thinking of the unhappy young girl, dismissed and marginalized, who referred to her childhood as "my prison of sadness." And I heard the words she said to me in those early days of our relationship: "It is my dream to become a doctor and to help the people of my country."

The ceremony began, and the university president soon began to call the name of each student. When he read slowly and deliberately "Elizabeth Rosita Cardona," Liz stood and walked up the steps onto the stage. The audience applauded, and I applauded loudest. A professor put a ribbon and a medal around Liz's neck, and she reached out to accept her cherished diploma. The university photographer took her picture with the president and a professor representing the school of medicine.

Tears lightly glazed in her eyes as she looked up into the crowd. Our eyes met, and I saw the biggest smile I had ever seen as she looked as if she were about to jump into the air. She mouthed words that touched my heart, words that I prayed would one day become a reality for her: "I did it, Mamita! I really did it!"

Everything from my past and present life felt small, insignificant, and trivial. Feeling content, with tears in my eyes and a full heart for the girl who taught me so many of life's greatest lessons, I waved to her fiercely. *Indeed you did, Liz. Indeed you did!*

# CHAPTER 32

# Condors Flying Free

The Andean condor is considered the largest flying bird in the world. It lives and soars on the seacoasts of South America and is particularly astonishing to see flying over Colca Canyon in Southern Peru. Its wingspan can reach up to ten and a half feet, and it can weigh up to thirty-three pounds. It is the world's largest raptor.

Every two years, the female makes a nest of twigs and branches high in a cave or the crevice of a mountainside. There, she lays a single egg. Both parents protect and nurture the baby chick until it is able to fly and often stay with the chick until it is several years old.

The Andean condors, though endangered, are fierce fighters and survivors. As such, they are an icon of this story. Liz also fought for her survival and achieved her greatest goal. And she may yet do great things.

———•═•◦•═•———

Following Liz's graduation, Tom and I wanted to visit Colca Canyon, about one hundred miles northwest of Arequipa. The canyon is one of the deepest in the world and is known as the habitat of the giant Andean condor. It is one of the most visited and spectacular attractions in Peru, where activities include river rafting, hiking, and photographing the magnificent condors in flight.

Carlos made arrangements with a friend who had a van and who agreed to drive us to Chivay, the town close by the canyon where we planned to stay the night. Our hotel in Arequipa had a hotel in Chivay, so we made reservations for three rooms for one night—one for Tom and me, one for Liz, and a third for Carlos.

We left around eight o'clock the following morning. The 150-mile road from Juliaca to Arequipa was tame compared to the twisting and sometime dirt road to Chivay. The van owner must have been used to this drive because he moved right along, only exaggerating the tossing and mobility of his passengers. But no one complained, least of all me. I sat in my seat, bumping up and down, which seemed to never stop. I shut my eyes, which helped make the road feel less bumpy, and thought that an important dream had just come true. I saw Liz graduate medical school with the highest respect and honor of her professors, her colleagues, and herself. She had received rave reviews on her thesis and had a bright future. I wasn't sure yet what Liz's not completing the SERUMS meant or the rationale for her decision, but she had completed medical school and was confident about her future. No longer would she have no coins in her purse. I felt proud, and that pride had nothing to do with the money it took to make it happen. *She did it!* And now she could fly free like the condors we hoped to see. With my eyes still closed, I reached over to her and squeezed her hand. She saw I had my closed eyes but that I was smiling. She whispered to me, "I love you, Mamita."

Mercifully, our driver stopped periodically. Once was to visit with a natively dressed woman with her llama and several baby llamas who stood by the roadside. We greeted the woman, pet her baby llamas, took photos, and gave the woman some coins. Where, I wondered had this person come from? There were no homes nearby. Where did she live? We arrived in Chivay by midafternoon, located the Casa Andina hotel, and checked into our adjacent rooms, which were clean and pleasant. "I feel like I'm still in the van, bouncing and flailing about!" I laughed as I kicked off my shoes and fell onto the bed.

In late afternoon, we all met in the hotel's foyer, where we decided to explore Chivay before finding a place for dinner. A while later, in the center of town, we wandered through a crowded farmer's market. Liz was behind Tom and saw a local woman reach into his back pocket and take his wallet. "Stop! You are stealing!" Liz shouted in Spanish as she yanked Tom's wallet from the woman's hand. We all watched the thief run away through the crowd of shoppers.

"My gosh, Liz!" I shouted. "How did you see that?"

"I didn't even feel it!" Tom reacted.

"People who pick the pockets are not uncommon," Liz said sadly. Then the protective condor parent told her offspring, "Tom, you need to keep your wallet in your front pocket or in Liz's purse, and pay attention to people who are around you."

Soon we found a small outdoor restaurant surrounded by tiki lights with Peruvian music playing softly. A waitress beckoned us to a table. A menu was on the wall. Tom and Carlos ordered a beer, and Liz and I had glasses of white wine. We all ordered the saltado with beef and peppers served on rice with, of course, french fries on top.

"This is a wonderful ending to the true celebration of your graduation from medical school, Liz," Tom said. "You said that you knew some doctors in Lima. Has anything come of that?"

"Yes, it has," she responded with excitement. "A gynecologist in his own clinic wants me to work with him. He wants me to examine patients, document the history and medications, and then get the patient ready for surgery, which the doctor will perform in the hospital. After surgery I would also see the patient for all postoperative examinations, prescribe medications, and discharge them." Liz sounded excited about this opportunity, especially since she didn't need to complete SERUMS for this job and could begin to practice right away.

After dinner the four of us walked around Chivay and then retired early. The next morning, after an early breakfast at Casa Andina, we drove to see the canyon and, hopefully, the condors, which were said to fly along the canyons in the early morning.

Along a walking path, for good luck, Liz and I stopped to make a small five-rock cairn, an art form of small stones balancing on each other. As we built our cairn tower, condors, with their wings flapping loudly, flew freely above us and over the canyon's traditional villages and ancient terraced agriculture plots. Everyone around us gazed in awe at the magnificent birds, and I thought about how they owned this canyon and we were their guests for just this moment.

"I want to fly free like that condor," Liz said as she jumped into the air.

Standing next to her, I hugged her and said, "You *are*, Liz. Now you can fly free. Nothing can stop you. You have put the sadness of your past behind you, and now you are free to fly like the condor." I was almost shouting.

As we finished our tower, Liz said, "Now we must together place the smallest top stone. That is the part for the good luck." I obeyed, and we placed the smallest stone on top. "There," she said. "Now this cairn tower will stand here forever and remember that we made this together at this very important moment in time." We hugged each other. I wondered if our small stone tower would stand as a memory of the time we shared together.

While we were making the tower, I noticed on Liz's third finger of her left hand a small silver ring with some stones on it. I had never seen her wear any jewelry, and I asked her what the ring was and where she got it.

"These are just fake stones. My girlfriend Pilar from my classes gave it to me as a present when we graduated last year before we did our internship," Liz said without eye contact. I took a closer look and decided that it was costume jewelry. On our bumpy return to Arequipa, the ring bothered me, and although she didn't seem to want to talk about it, I decided to do some asking.

"Are you still in touch with the man you met online who came to Arequipa to see you last year? I think you said his name was James."

"Yes, dear Liz, I hear from him sometimes, but we are just friends."

"What did you say he did? I forgot," I lied.

"He studied accounting and now works for a company as an accountant." she replied as she smiled and looked at the ring.

"Does he have family and friends?" I asked, hoping to get more information.

"He said he has a sister and some friends from work."

"In the US," I said, "most married women wear wedding rings on their third finger of the left hand. Like mine—see? Is that not the case in Peru?"

"Here it can be either way. This ring from Pilar fits better on my left hand," she responded, still without eye contact.

When we arrived at the Casa Andina in Arequipa, it was time to say goodbye. Liz and Carlos were leaving the following day for Lima and her new job at the gynecology clinic. Carlos would return to work at a bank in Lima. Tom and I would head home to New Mexico. We all were teary eyed.

"Liz," she said to me, "we will see each other again. I know we will. Nothing can ever break the bond that we have. I do not want to cry because I want to think about all that you have helped me to accomplish and all that we have brought into our lives."

"Yes, Liz," I said softly.

We all hugged and parted. As Tom and I started to walk into our hotel, I let Tom go ahead of me. I watched Liz and Carlos walk down Jerusalem Street side by side. Where they were headed, I did not know. When we parted, I wondered if this might be my last glimpses of the woman who had put so much of her hurtful past behind her and was truly ready to fly free like the condor.

# EPILOGUE

Liz and I continued to email and periodically talk on the phone. She said she was living in Lima and working for a gynecologist in his office in a lovely part of the city. She was being paid, of course, and she had a small apartment with all the necessities. Carlos worked at a bank and bused to Arequipa frequently to see his daughters.

Our conversations were cheerful, and we often laughed about some of the fun things we had done together in Peru. I asked her if she had made any more of the lomo saltado with the yellow "papers" and how they tasted. We reminisced about the Arequipa earthquake in 2005 when I was working in the hospital among screaming children and mothers and she and Tom were stopped in a taxi at a red light while the earth shook. I said I had gotten the short straw on the deal. We laughed, although I had to explain the idiom. We reminisced about our day in Colca Canyon, building our cairn tower and watching the condors in flight overhead. Over the next few months, we talked every couple of weeks. Early in May 2010, I wasn't able to reach Liz by phone and she didn't answer my emails. I was a bit concerned but also knew that she was deep into her work.

Tom and I flew to Minnesota later that month to visit family and friends, play golf, and enjoy some favorite restaurants and sights in the Twin Cities. We rented a car, and Jenny and Mike invited us to stay with them and their three young boys at their home in Wayzata. Mike owns the Fish Guys, a distributor of fine seafood, so dinners in Wayzata were amazing when Mike served such delicacies as huge shrimp cocktails and Jenny prepared wild Alaskan halibut cheeks.

Our vacation included restful mornings, except for one. Near the end of our visit, at eleven o'clock am central time on Wednesday, May 26, my cell phone rang, and it was Liz. She sounded happy and glad that I picked up. We exchanged the usual greetings.

Then I asked, "How's your work at the clinic? I haven't heard from you for a while, so I'm betting you are busy and enjoying working with your doctors."

"Well, Mamita Liz," she said softly, "I am no longer in Peru. I am living in Maple Grove, Minnesota. I am married to James, the man I told you about who came to see me in Arequipa."

I sank onto a bar stool in Jenny's kitchen. "What? Liz, When did this happen?" I asked.

"James did all the paperwork and made all the arrangements so I could come to the US during my summer break in January 2009. We were married then. After a few days, I returned to Peru to complete the intern year, you remember," Liz said.

I was stunned. Liz said they were living in James's trailer in Maple Grove on the north side of Minneapolis. She didn't have a job. She said James worked as an accountant.

"Liz," I said, "I don't know what to say, but I know that I'm disappointed that you didn't tell me this at the time it happened. So, you got married *before* you did your internship? If you were married before you did the internship, then why wasn't James involved in paying your internship and graduation costs, and why wasn't he at your graduation? And what now has happened to your dream to help your people, Liz?" I was upset, but I tried not to shout. *What* has *happened to her dream?* My thoughts were racing.

Liz had left Peru, had no job, and hadn't done the SERUMS. She hadn't completed any requirements to become licensed as a doctor in the US. *What was she thinking? What has she done?*

"I have learned from friends that I can study and take an exam to help me get a residency here in the US," Liz said.

"Well, yes," I said. "I think that's possible. But there are prearrangements and many steps to be taken to be accepted in a residency here in the US. It's complicated. A doctor from a foreign country is usually sponsored or has arrangements with a practice, hospital, or medical school that permits the new doctor to work and observe before taking an exam, which may lead to a residency program. Then there are still US training and medical board exams required in order to practice legally in the US. You told Tom and me that you wanted to be a doctor in Peru. What happened to that?"

I told Liz I would call her back later. I was upset and had to digest all that she had just said.

When Liz and I said goodbye, I said to Tom, "Oh, my God, You won't believe this."

I explained what Liz had said, and we talked for a half hour. My niece, Jenny, who knew the story, was included in our conversations. Tom was staying in Minnesota for several more days to see his children, and I was scheduled to fly back to New Mexico the following morning. When I told Tom about this conversation, he said, "Contact Liz again and ask her if I can take her and James to dinner maybe tomorrow evening. I'm flying back to New Mexico on Saturday, but I'd like to meet them both."

I called Liz on her cell and tried to be cheery. I explained that I would be leaving the following day to go home but that Tom wanted to see her and James and take them out for a congratulatory dinner before he left Minneapolis. He wanted my conversation to be upbeat so they would accept.

"That would be nice, Mamita," Liz responded enthusiastically. "I will arrange the dinner at a restaurant nearby. I will let you know."

I left Jenny and Mike's home and returned to Las Cruces. A day or two later, Tom met Liz and her husband at a restaurant. James, Tom said, was bubbly, ebullient. He seemed proud of what he had accomplished—marrying a soon-to-be American doctor. When asked about his work, James, Tom said, described himself as a billing clerk. Meanwhile, Liz sat mostly silent with her hands folded, staring into her lap as James waxed enthusiastic. "Oh my," Tom said when he called later that evening, "what have these two gotten themselves into?"

In the weeks and months that followed, Liz and I communicated, but the tone of our conversations were flat. I asked what she was planning to do. Did she, and did James, think that because she had graduated medical school in Peru that she could easily become a doctor in the United States? *What is wrong here?* I kept asking myself.

In an email and on the phone, she confessed that she was unhappy. She said sadly and softly, "I know now that I made a mistake. James told me in the beginning that he would help me find work and pay for me to have the schooling and any training I needed to apply for the medical tests and complete a medical residency. None of that has happened." James was not in the health care business, so it was hard to imagine what he could do to help Liz find work in a medical career. Such help was not forthcoming.

I said to Liz, "Maybe it's not too late. What if you call Dr. Jacinta Torres at your college and ask her—beg her—to let you back in to the university so you can start the SERUMS. I will pay for your flight back to Arequipa. Liz, you must think about this seriously because there is no hope for you to become a doctor here unless you get into a residency program. You have no connections in Minnesota to make this happen. I'm not in Minnesota any longer, although perhaps I could help you in New Mexico, where your language would be a huge asset. All this could take a long time. It would be much better if you returned to Peru and finished the SERUMS," I said.

"You just don't want me to be happy. You don't care about my happiness," she said.

This was new. "Liz," I said, "that was the whole point of your becoming a doctor! You have the brains and smarts to do this, and I helped you for six years so you *can be happy,* not live in poverty, *and* help your people. It is what you have said you wanted all along."

Then I suggested, "Why don't you put on your business suit and go to any Minneapolis hospital and clinic human resources department. Ask for a face-to-face interview with someone in HR to whom you can tell your medical school story and fill out an application and bring all your documents. Personal contact is always the best way to get your foot in the door."

"I can't do that because I can't drive and James has to work," she responded.

"Well, you said James agreed to help you. He decided to bring you here, and now he should help you find a job in a health care field where you can try to get to know people who may be able to help you," I said firmly.

Liz found a couple of what proved to be short-term jobs, one cleaning rooms at a hotel. She said it was horrible and was fired after two days. "This work is for mules," she told me. I made a trip to Minneapolis in July, and Liz had arranged an appointment online at a private research facility associated with the University of Minnesota for a research assistant position in the medical research department.

*Great*, I thought. "How about I take you to that interview?" I said.

I drove Liz to the interview and waited in the parking lot for nearly an hour. *Maybe that's a good sign. They haven't said, "Go away."* She came out and said it "went well," but the woman who interviewed her said her lack of research experience might not be a good fit. I asked her the woman's name and her title. She didn't know. I suggested that, going forward, she write down the names of people and the titles of everyone with whom she interviews. Then, following the interview, she should send a handwritten thank you note or an e-mail. I told her this is basic business courtesy when interviewing.

She didn't get an offer from the university. The next job she found was at minimum wage assembling cell phones on a night shift. It was a long way from where she and James lived. Still, James drove her to work and picked her up afterward. After a couple of years, she applied for and was accepted for a position as an intake clerk at a local clinic. A year or so later, she became a medical coding clerk. Her bilingual skills definitely helped, but I never received a clear story about exactly what she was doing. As time went on in our occasional conversations, she said she was an analyst, advising clinicians and doctors, establishing diagnoses, creating plans of care, and ordering lab reports. These activities are the responsibilities of licensed physicians, although often in conjunction with other licensed personnel such as nurse practitioners or physician's assistants. I hoped she was not overstepping her boundaries. I asked her once if she was disappointed that she was not a licensed physician in the United States. She did not like that question and responded, "I am providing a good service, and I'm helping people and doctors, and that is what I want to do." *So be it*, I thought. That is indeed what she said she wanted to do.

It was now 2012, nearly eight years after Liz and I met on that morning in June 2004 in Arequipa. Although our lives were meshed together and we continued to have occasional conversations, I was confused, disappointed and angry. I had begun to write our story early on, as it unfolded, but now I was discouraged and saw no way that I could bring it to an end. I set aside my Liz Cardona Story and focused on my part-time business as a legal medical consultant working with attorneys on their medical malpractice, personal injury, and wrongful death cases. In 2016, my legal work lightened. Tom suggested that because I'd had time to distance myself, it might be satisfying to return to this book. And he was right. As I reread the draft manuscript I had written between 2004 and 2010, I realized that I was more open minded and my anger and hurtfulness was gone. I still knew that poverty, social class, culture, and Liz's stubbornness and passion for her own freedom to fly were all playing a part in my story of Liz and me. I was proud that she wanted to fly her own course in life, but felt that her stubbornness may have gotten in her way of common sense thinking and that her choosing a man who promised her a better way of life had clouded her vision for pursuing her medical dreams. Liz's stubbornness to blend in is one of the qualities that helped her through medical school when the majority of her classmates came from wealthy families and Liz was an outsider. I know that she had to stand up for herself to her colleagues and to the doctors. Meanwhile, she told me during infrequent conversations that she continued to prepare for the examinations that would lead to a US residency. When Liz first came to the United States, she told me that she had met several other foreign doctors who, like her were studying for residency exams. Each time we talked, I asked her when she would take those tests. I told her I thought she would pass them because they would cover material she had learned recently. One day she scheduled and took the exam unsuccessfully, a few days later we had a tearful talk. She was late to the exam because James, who drove her, didn't know the location well. Time ran out before she could finish, and she was excused. She could retake the exam, but in later conversations she was evasive. I began to feel that these were excuses. While Liz was a good student and could stand up for herself, she seemed unable to pull the triggers to make things happen in this situation.

For a couple of years, after she rejected the idea of returning to Peru for the SERUMS, I tried to find a way for her to practice in the United States. I asked physicians I had come to know in New Mexico for suggestions and talked with local hospitals, as well as the medical school at the University of Texas in El Paso. Everyone was encouraging because the need for bilingual physicians in the southwest United States is great.

People were interested in meeting Liz and wanted to help. But when I told Liz about these opportunities, she declined.

Then there is the issue of expectations. Did Liz think she could easily transfer her medical degree from Peru to the United States? And did James also think that in a snap Liz could become a practicing US physician? I began to question who might have deceived whom, intentionally or not. I also wondered if she assumed, having visited us over the holidays in 2005, that prosperity comes easily in the United States. The other thought I had was that perhaps Liz really could not cope with the responsibility of being a practicing doctor. Perhaps she couldn't or wouldn't do the SERUMS because she couldn't cope with the responsibility. Perhaps it was because the memory of her childhood in Aplao haunted her. The answers were and still are unknown to me.

I am certain Liz was genuine in her desire to become a doctor in Peru, and she clearly demonstrated her ability to succeed. She graduated medical school. But what happened to her goal of helping her people? We could never have predicted that James would enter the equation and redirect Liz's plans. Certainly medical students the world over change their minds and become less altruistic as school grinds on and debts increase. Sometimes I think that Liz was influenced by her wealthier classmates, who began to talk of going to other countries to make more money than they could in Peru. Her good friend Jorge planned to do the SERUMS in Peru and then go to Argentina, where he had already been accepted for a residency. Perhaps Liz thought that by marrying James he could offer a ticket to such financial success for both of them in the United States.

I doubt I will ever know the true answers to these questions. I have an amiable relationship with Liz that I hope to sustain. I know that when we have had tough conversations about her work, her goals, and what she wants to do to follow through with her dream, she does not call me. After several months, I call her. I do not want to lose contact with her, and I believe she feels the same.

We never really know how our life plans will turn out. We can speculate, we can guess, and we can hope, but nothing is guaranteed. When Liz and I talk, she is usually the one to say, "Mamita, we are connected so much. We have a bond. I will always love what you and Papito Tom have done for me." She is sincere.

I do not know how this story will end and probably never will. I do know a couple of things: I know that Liz was a poor girl with little hope for a successful future. I know she wanted to be a doctor with all her heart and to help her people. I know that she accomplished this; she graduated medical school. I know my help allowed her to do it. Liz Cardona will write the ending to her own story. I do know that I would do it all again. And I know that Liz Cardona was born to be a condor flying free.

And perhaps one day she will.